AMERICAN
WAR LIBRARY

★ ★ ★ ★

★ The War on Terrorism ★

WEAPONS OF WAR

by Craig E. Blohm

LUCENT
BOOKS®

THOMSON
───────★───────™
GALE

San Diego • Detroit • New York • San Francisco • Cleveland • New Haven, Conn. • Waterville, Maine • London • Munich

In memory of my brother,
Jeffrey A. Blohm.

LIBRARY OF CONGRESS CATALOGING-IN-PUBLICATION DATA

Blohm, Craig E., 1948–
    Weapons of war / by Craig E. Blohm.
        v. cm.—(American war library, the war on terrorism)
    Includes bibliographical references and index.
    Contents: How will we fight and win this war?—Organizing for battle—Air attack
over Afghanistan—Bombs and missiles—Support aircraft and helicopters—
Gathering intelligence—Special-operations forces—Ground war weapons.
        ISBN 1-59018-332-0 (hardback : alk. paper)
    1. United States—Armed Forces—Weapons systems. 2. War on Terrorism, 2001—
Equipment and supplies. [1. United States—Armed Forces—Weapons systems. 2. War
on Terrorism, 2001–] I. Title. II. American war library. War on terrorism series
        UF503.B56 2004
        958.104'6—dc21
                                                                                    2003003538

Printed in the United States of America

⋆ **Contents** ⋆

Foreword 5

Introduction: "How Will We Fight and Win This War?" 7

Chapter 1: Organizing for Battle. 10

Chapter 2: Air Attack over Afghanistan 22

Chapter 3: Bombs and Missiles 35

Chapter 4: Support Aircraft and Helicopters 48

Chapter 5: Gathering Intelligence 60

Chapter 6: Special-Operations Forces. 73

Chapter 7: Ground War Weapons. 86

Notes 98

For Further Reading 102

Works Consulted 103

Index 107

Picture Credits. 111

About the Author 112

A Nation Forged by War

The United States, like many nations, was forged and defined by war. Despite Benjamin Franklin's opinion that "There never was a good war or a bad peace," the United States owes its very existence to the War of Independence, one to which Franklin wholeheartedly subscribed. The country forged by war in 1776 was tempered and made stronger by the Civil War in the 1860s.

The Texas Revolution, the Mexican-American War, and the Spanish-American War expanded the country's borders and gave it overseas possessions. These wars made the United States a world power, but this status came with a price, as the nation became a key but reluctant player in both World War I and World War II.

Each successive war further defined the country's role on the world stage. Following World War II, U.S. foreign policy redefined itself to focus on the role of defender, not only of the freedom of its own citizens, but also of the freedom of people everywhere. During the Cold War that followed World War II until the collapse of the Soviet Union, defending the world meant fighting communism. This goal, manifested in the Korean and Vietnam conflicts, proved elusive, and soured the American public on its achievability. As the United States emerged as the world's sole superpower, American foreign policy has been guided less by national interest and more by protecting international human rights. But as involvement in Somalia and Kosovo prove, this goal has been equally elusive.

As a result, the country's view of itself changed. Bolstered by victories in World Wars I and II, Americans first relished the role of protector. But, as war followed war in a seemingly endless procession, Americans began to doubt their leaders, their motives, and themselves. The Vietnam War especially caused people to question the validity of sending its young people to die in places where they were not particularly wanted and for people who did not seem especially grateful.

While the most obvious changes brought about by America's wars have been geopolitical in nature, many other aspects of society have been touched. War often does not bring about change directly, but acts instead like the catalyst in a chemical reaction, accelerating changes already in progress.

Some of these changes have been societal. The role of women in the United States had been slowly changing, but World War II put thousands into the workforce and into uniform. They might have gone back to being housewives after the war, but equality, once experienced, would not be forgotten.

Likewise, wars have accelerated technological change. The necessity for faster airplanes and more destructive bombs led to the development of jet planes and nuclear energy. Artificial fibers developed for parachutes in the 1940s were used in clothing of the 1950s.

Lucent Books' American War Library covers key wars in the development of the nation. Each war is covered in several volumes, to allow for more detail, context, and to provide volumes on often neglected subjects, such as the kamikazes of World War II, or the weapons used in the Civil War. As with all Lucent books, notes, annotated bibliographies, and appendixes such as glossaries give students a launching point for further research. In addition, sidebars and archival photographs enhance the text. Together, each volume in The American War Library will aid students in understanding how America's wars have shaped and changed its politics, economics, and society.

"How Will We Fight and Win This War?"

The airplanes came out of a clear blue sky. At first, witnesses on the ground could not quite believe what they were seeing as they watched dense black smoke rising into the morning sky. The sounds of sirens filled the air and people ran, some to help, others to escape the devastation that the aircraft had wrought. The attack had been a complete surprise, although later many people would say that the government had known, or at least should have known, that the United States was vulnerable. A few even said that the government had allowed the attack to happen as an excuse to go to war. In any case, the reaction to the catastropic destruction and loss of thousands of lives was clear: Americans called for immediate and decisive military action to punish those responsible.

Most people immediately associate this description with the events of September 11, 2001, when terrorists hijacked four commercial airliners and sent them hurtling into the World Trade Center towers in New York City, the Pentagon in Washington, D.C., and a Pennsylvania field. In fact, these words also accurately describe the events of December 7, 1941, when aircraft of the Imperial Japanese Navy attacked the U.S. naval base at Pearl Harbor, Hawaii, sinking or damaging twenty-one ships and killing more than twenty-four hundred people. Many similarities are evident, but fundamental differences in the two attacks made what followed dramatically different as well.

A New Kind of Enemy

Both attacks caused huge damage and killed thousands. Both caught the United States by surprise, and both led America into wars: Pearl Harbor forced the U.S. entry into World War II, while September 11 gave rise to the coordinated military campaigns and official domestic programs collectively known as the war on terrorism. But there the similarities end. For our adversary in the war on terrorism is by its nature a different kind of enemy, hiding in the world's political shadows and making targets of the innocent and unsuspecting. In World War II our enemy was clearly defined: the Axis powers led by Germany and Japan. But in the war on terrorism, the enemy is not so easily identified. Terrorists conceal their identities, show allegiance to no nation, wear no uniforms, and fight not over land or wealth but for a radical ideology that to many of their victims seems incomprehensible. Terrorists do not assemble a single unified army, but build instead a worldwide underground network to spread their terror, then fade into the background to regroup and strike another day.

The World Trade Center's south tower explodes from the impact of the second plane as the north tower smolders.

Did America have the means to defeat such an elusive foe? As President George W. Bush stated in an address to Congress and the nation, "Americans are asking: How will we fight and win this war?"[1]

New Tactics and New Weapons

Throughout the modern era of warfare, the United States has been in the forefront of weapons design. In World War II airpower proved its worth as the U.S. Army Air Force pounded Germany with high-explosive munitions and ended the war with atomic bombs. The aircraft carrier replaced the venerable battleship as the most potent weapon in the naval fleet. On the ground, U.S. tanks rumbled through Europe and infantry units liberated occupied towns and villages. In the postwar conflicts of Korea, Vietnam, and the 1991 Persian Gulf War, these basic weapons were joined by new ones, including intercontinental ballistic missiles, nuclear submarines, and "smart" bombs. All these weapons were designed to fight a conventional war against a conventional enemy; that is, an enemy with an army, navy, and air force equipped with similar weaponry and using similar strategies and tactics. After September 11, 2001, when America's latest foe turned out to be a terrorist organization known as al-Qaeda, U.S. military leaders began to think of how best to employ its weapons.

The war on terrorism would be a different kind of war. "This war," said Bush, "will not be like the [Persian Gulf] war against Iraq a decade ago, with a decisive liberation of territory and a swift conclusion. . . . Our response involves far more than instant retaliation and isolated strikes. Americans should not expect one battle, but a lengthy campaign, unlike any other we have ever seen."[2] The president vowed to seek out terrorists wherever they were found and to punish those who harbored them. The first object of American might would be Afghanistan, where the ruling regime known as the Taliban gave refuge and support to al-Qaeda terrorists.

Along with the traditional aircraft and ships, the war on terrorism would include some new weapons. Some of these high-tech marvels had seen limited use before, while others would be rushed to completion and tested in the heat of battle. Lasers would guide bombs and missiles to their targets with pinpoint accuracy. Soldiers would be able to see in the dark with night-vision goggles. Global Positioning System satellites orbiting high above Earth would tell field commanders where they were and, more importantly, where the enemy was. And planes without pilots would transmit television pictures of the battlefield to generals halfway around the world.

As at the beginning of any war, none of America's generals or admirals really knew how the battles would play out in the weeks and months ahead of them. What they did know, however, was that the United States had the best-trained and best-equipped soldiers in the world, and the best weapons available would be brought to bear in Operation Enduring Freedom, in Afghanistan, the first battleground in the war on terrorism.

Chapter 1

Organizing for Battle

A fghanistan, a nation in southern Asia, is just slightly smaller in area than the state of Texas. It is a rough land of arid plains and rugged mountains dotted with innumerable caves. Afghanistan is virtually without water within its own borders, a landlocked nation surrounded by Iran, Pakistan, and the former Soviet republics of Tajikistan, Uzbekistan, and Turkmenistan. Located more than six thousand miles from the United States, one can think of few places more difficult than Afghanistan in which to wage a war. "It is difficult for me to imagine how Americans can fight here,"[3] remarked a local Afghan military commander. But when terrorists, trained in the al-Qaeda terror camps in Afghanistan, attacked the World Trade Center and the Pentagon on September 11, 2001, they brought their particularly despicable brand of war to the United States. Within days of these attacks, however, U.S. plans for a counterstrike were under way. Soon it would be time for America to bring the war to Afghanistan.

A Global Response

On September 20, 2001, President George W. Bush addressed a joint session of Congress and, via radio and television, the American people. In an eloquent speech, Bush praised the bravery of rescue workers, encouraged Americans still in shock from the attacks, and described the elusive enemy that the United States was now up against. He then made a public announcement to America's soldiers, sailors, and airmen: "Tonight, a few miles from the damaged Pentagon, I have a message for our military: Be ready. I've called the Armed Forces to alert, and there is a reason. The hour is coming when America will act, and you will make us proud."[4] In fact, on September 12, the day after the terrorist attacks, Secretary of Defense Donald Rumsfeld had ordered the preparation of "credible military options"[5] to the growing threat of global terrorism. And just before he gave his speech to Congress, Bush, as commander in chief of the U.S. armed forces, officially told his military leaders to get ready for war.

But what kind of war would it be? The Soviet Army spent nearly ten years fighting a guerrilla war to support a pro-Soviet government in Afghanistan. But even after putting more than six hundred thousand troops on the ground, they were forced to leave in 1989. According to General Tommy R. Franks, the commander of U.S. military operations in Afghanistan, "We took that as instructive—as a way not to do it."[6] The

General Tommy R. Franks: Leading the War on Terrorism

Just as a movie has one director and an orchestra one conductor, Operation Enduring Freedom, the military response to the September 11, 2001, terrorist attacks, had one supreme commander: U.S. Army general Tommy R. Franks. Tall and lean with the bearing and rugged features of a career soldier, Franks, a native of Wynnewood, Oklahoma, was commissioned as a second lieutenant in 1967. After serving a tour in Vietnam and subsequent duty in artillery battalions, Franks was assigned to the Pentagon in 1976, where he served in the investigations division and in the office of the chief of staff.

During his army career Franks earned undergraduate and graduate degrees as well as attending the Armed Forces Staff College and the Army War College. He saw action in the Persian Gulf War as assistant division commander (maneuver) of the First Cavalry Division. In June 2000 he received a promotion to general and became the commander in chief of United States Central Command (CENTCOM).

Franks is an outspoken general who is not afraid to express his opinion in a brusque manner. Often compared to General Norman Schwarzkopf, the U.S. military commander in the Persian Gulf War, Franks sometimes comes out on the short end of the comparison. Unlike "Stormin' Norman," Franks displays a low-key demeanor and appears somewhat ill at ease at press conferences. Early in Operation Enduring Freedom some criticized Franks for not pursuing the bombing campaign more aggressively or putting in ground troops sooner. But the swift fall of the Taliban proved the merit of General Franks's conservative approach in the war on terrorism.

Even before September 11, 2001, the general had already displayed some insight into the world of terrorism, as reported by Duncan Campbell of the British newspaper, the *Guardian* (www.guardian.co.uk). Franks said, "I don't believe that the threat has been exaggerated. I believe that it is possible for very small numbers of committed terrorists to bring great instability and a sense of insecurity to people in the region."

General Tommy R. Franks commanded all facets of Operation Enduring Freedom.

United States would fight its war in Afghanistan by beginning with an all-out aerial bombardment of Taliban and al-Qaeda training camps, radar facilities, aircraft, and other vital military assets. This first phase would be followed by units of U.S. Special Forces fighting alongside local anti-Taliban forces known as the Northern Alliance to wipe out any further resistance.

But preparing for a massive air assault six thousand miles from the United States posed several challenges for President Bush and his military commanders.

Staging for War

Conducting a major military campaign in a foreign land requires transporting men, equipment, and ammunition to staging areas in the theater of operation. For Operation Enduring Freedom, the name given to the war against terrorism, this meant bringing U.S. war machinery, especially combat aircraft, to the volatile region of the Middle East. But many nations in the region were hesitant to cooperate with U.S. military leaders. "In the initial phase of the operation," comments Milan Vego, a professor at the Naval War College, "the U.S. military lacked adequate host-nation support to insert its ground forces and land-based aircraft into the area adjacent to Afghanistan."[7]

Saudi Arabia, a nation that had long been friendly to the United States, refused

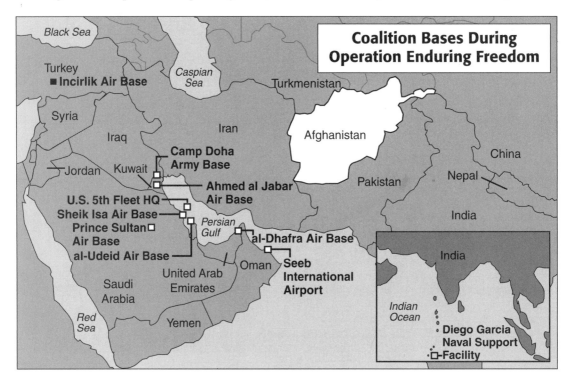

Coalition Bases During Operation Enduring Freedom

Forming a Coalition

When terrorists crashed two airliners into New York's World Trade Center on September 11, 2001, innocent people from more than eighty countries died in the destruction of the twin towers. It is fitting, then, that the war on terrorism would be carried out by an international coalition of nations providing economic, intelligence, and military assistance to Operation Enduring Freedom. President George W. Bush gave a televised speech to Congress nine days after the attacks (the entire text of his speech can be found on the White House website at www.whitehouse.gov). Speaking to America and the world, Bush said, "This is not, however, just America's fight. And what is at stake is not just America's freedom. This is the world's fight. . . . The United States is grateful that many nations and many international organizations have already responded—with sympathy and with support. . . . The civilized world is rallying to America's side. They understand that if this terror goes unpunished, their own cities, their own citizens may be next. Terror, unanswered, can not only bring down buildings, it can threaten the stability of legitimate governments."

One year after the terrorist attacks, some ninety nations were supporting the war on terrorism. Their assistance ranged from seizing terrorist assets and granting overflight permission for combat aircraft, to providing special-operations troops for the ground war in Afghanistan. Thirty-seven nations from five continents actually provided military forces to Operation Enduring Freedom.

to let the U.S. Air Force conduct flights from the Prince Sultan Air Base about seventy miles south of Riyadh. This was in line with a ten-year-old Saudi policy of forbidding the United States to launch offensive air strikes from an air installation in Saudi Arabia. The United States was, however, allowed to use the Prince Sultan Air Base as a command-and-control center for coordinating the air war over Afghanistan. Other U.S. bases in Oman, Qatar, Kuwait, and on Diego Garcia, an island in the Indian Ocean, would also be used for the war in Afghanistan. But providing facilities for launching the massive air strikes anticipated would take more than the few available land bases. U.S. military planners looked to the world's oceans and the mighty force that patrolled them: the U.S. Navy.

". . . From the Sea"

During the Cold War, U.S. military and political strategy centered on a doctrine known as containment, which sought to limit the Soviet Union's ability to spread communism around the world. But with the dissolution of the Soviet Union in 1989 the United States had to redefine how its military might could best be used in the post–Cold War era. While a global war fought with ballistic missiles launched from U.S. or Soviet soil was now less likely, the United States had to demonstrate to the world that its military was still a force to be reckoned with. The resulting concept of "forward presence" called for U.S. forces to be visibly deployed in areas of the world where the United States had vital interests. U.S. troops stationed in Europe, the Middle East, and other potential hot spots served as a demonstration of U.S. commitment in those regions. But since the end of the Cold War many U.S. bases overseas have been closed. And while land-based installations are necessary for the security of American interests overseas, few things present quite so impressive a visual statement of military might as a U.S. warship.

The U.S. Navy stated its post–Cold War strategic concept in an official report entitled ". . . From the Sea: Preparing the Naval Service for the 21st Century":

> Our strategy has shifted from a focus on a global threat to a focus on regional challenges and opportunities. While the prospect of a global war has receded, we are entering a period of enormous uncertainty in regions critical to our national interests. . . . Our naval forces will be full participants in the principal elements of this strategy—strategic deterrence and defense, forward presence, crisis response, and reconstitution.[8]

U.S. Navy warships are an ideal vehicle for carrying out the task of forward presence. On station all over the world, they can be deployed quickly in time of crisis. Huge aircraft carriers and heavily armed destroyers and cruisers are highly visible to the people and leaders of foreign nations. In addition, U.S. naval vessels do not depend on a foreign host nation for support but are considered sovereign territory of the United States. In the wake of the attacks of September 11, 2001, U.S. attention turned to Afghanistan, the source and protector of the al-Qaeda terrorists. Unfortunately for the terrorists, not even a landlocked nation like Afghanistan can escape the reach of the U.S. Navy.

Where Are the Carriers?

Aircraft carriers have played a decisive role in U.S. military operations since World War II and are now the navy's primary weapon of forward presence and crisis response. President Bill Clinton, on a visit to the carrier USS *Theodore Roosevelt* in March 1993 said, "When word of a crisis breaks out in Washington, it's no accident that the first question that comes to everyone's lips is: 'Where is the nearest carrier?'"[9] In October 2001 the USS *Theodore Roosevelt* was one of five U.S. aircraft carriers that took part in Operation Enduring Freedom.

When the terrorists struck, one of those carriers was on its way toward the Arabian Sea to take part in Operation Southern Watch, a mission to provide aircraft for patrolling the skies over Iraq. As the carrier rounded the tip of India and headed for its duty station, word came of the attacks on New York and Washington. At that moment the USS *Carl Vinson* began preparing to be a leading force in the war on terrorism in Afghanistan. A closer look at this mighty fighting vessel will provide an example of the kind of U.S. naval power brought to bear against the Taliban and al-Qaeda in Afghanistan.

Nuclear Carriers

Shortly after the end of World War II the U.S. Navy began to recognize the advantages of using nuclear energy to power naval vessels. Under nuclear propulsion a ship could travel great distances without refueling, and valuable space taken up by huge fuel tanks would be eliminated. Admiral Hyman Rickover, the "father of the nuclear navy," championed nuclear propulsion for ships. In January 1955, largely due to Rickover's tireless efforts, the world's first nuclear-powered ship, the submarine USS *Nautilus,* made its historic maiden voyage.

After the success of the *Nautilus,* the benefits of nuclear propulsion for enormous ships such as aircraft carriers soon became clear. A conventional oil-burning carrier had to carry more than eight thousand tons of fuel for each voyage and could use up to half this fuel in just a few days. Nuclear power eliminates the need for frequent oil replenishment from tanker ships, thus allowing a carrier to operate for years before replacing its nuclear fuel. In a nuclear-powered vessel, one or more nuclear reactors are used to produce heat that turns water in a closed piping system into steam. This steam is then directed through a turbine that turns the ship's propellers. When the steam condenses back into water, pumps return it to the reactor and the cycle repeats. Nuclear power is clean and efficient, and safety is always emphasized: Heavy shielding keeps the crew safe from the radioactivity in the reactors.

In November 1961 the world's first nuclear-powered aircraft carrier, the USS *Enterprise,* was commissioned. The "Big E" participated in the blockade of Cuba during the missile crisis of 1962 and played a combat role in the war in Vietnam. It would

The aircraft carrier USS Enterprise *was one of the first deployed in Operation Enduring Freedom.*

join Operation Enduring Freedom in September 2001. In May 1975 the first of a new class of nuclear-powered aircraft carriers, the USS *Nimitz*, was commissioned. The USS *Carl Vinson*, designated CVN-70 (CV for carrier and N for nuclear-powered), is one of nine Nimitz-class carriers that provide the backbone of the modern navy's forward-presence mission.

A City Afloat

Peterborough, New Hampshire, is a picturesque New England town with a population of about fifty-seven hundred people. Now imagine taking all the residents of Peterborough and putting them on a ship measuring 1,092 feet long and 250 feet wide, traveling the oceans of the world at a speed of more than thirty-five miles per hour. This gives you an idea of the number of people it takes to keep the USS *Carl Vinson* operat-

ing and ready to respond to any international crisis. Some other statistics may help to demonstrate the sheer size of this huge ship. At 250 feet from the keel to the top of its mast, the *Vinson* is as tall as a twenty-five-story building. New York's famed skyscraper, the Chrysler Building, if laid down horizontally on the *Vinson*, would not even reach the ends of the flight deck. At four and one-half acres in size, the deck encompasses almost as much area as four football fields. Below the flight deck is a bewildering array of more than a thousand compartments including crew quarters and dining areas, electronic and mechanical repair shops, machinery spaces, storerooms, a post office, medical and dental facilities, and even a fully equipped television studio. Nearly one thousand miles of wire, cable, and piping snake throughout the area belowdecks. Power to turn the *Vinson*'s four massive propellers is

Central Command

To protect America's interests around the globe, the U.S. military is divided into Unified Combatant Commands. Each command is an operational group that includes forces from two or more service branches and is usually organized geographically. There are currently nine Unified Combatant Commands; responsibility for the central Asian region, which includes Afghanistan, falls to the United States Central Command, or CENTCOM.

CENTCOM was created in response to the Soviet invasion of Afghanistan in 1979. It officially went into operation in 1983, headquartered at MacDill Air Force Base in Tampa, Florida. CENTCOM employs combat forces from the army, navy, air force, marines, and special operations. During Op-

eration Desert Storm in 1991, CENTCOM was led by General Norman Schwarzkopf. General Tommy Franks, CENTCOM's commander in chief during the war on terrorism, took over in June 2000.

CENTCOM's AOR, or Area of Responsibility, includes twenty-five diverse nations from Afghanistan, Iraq, and Uzbekistan to Egypt and Kenya. Its geographical territory encompasses an area larger than that of the continental United States. In this politically volatile region, CENTCOM represents a force of seventeen thousand to twenty-five thousand personnel deployed at any given time, with duties ranging from rapid response to humanitarian crises to maintaining a stabilizing forward presence to fighting the nation's wars.

provided by two nuclear reactors located on the lowest level of the carrier.

The USS *Carl Vinson*, like all *Nimitz*-class carriers, is an "angled-deck" carrier. On the aircraft carriers of World War II, one long, straight flight deck extending from the bow to the stern was used for all take-offs and landings. But with the advent of faster jet-powered aircraft after the war came the distinct possibility of a landing jet crashing into another aircraft waiting to take off. So new aircraft carriers were designed with a portion of the flight deck angled about fourteen degrees from the vessel's centerline and extending about two-thirds of the length of the ship. Incoming aircraft would land on the angled section while take-offs were made from two steam-powered catapults on the forward straight portion of the deck. This reduced the danger of crashes and allowed simultaneous takeoffs and landings. On the *Vinson* two additional catapults are located on the angled deck for launch operations when aircraft are not landing. Four massive elevators bring aircraft up to the flight deck from the hangar deck one level below.

Defensive Armament

Aircraft carriers do not bristle with guns like famous battleships of old. Their companion ships in the battle group, as well as the carrier's own planes, provide protection for the modern aircraft carrier. But carriers like the *Carl Vinson* do carry armament to defend against enemy attacks. The Mark 29 Sea Sparrow is a medium-range surface-to-air

The USS Carl Vinson *launches a Sea Sparrow missile.*

missile that the *Vinson* can fire to intercept incoming enemy aircraft or missiles. The twelve-foot-long, eight-inch-diameter missile is propelled by a solid-fuel rocket engine and carries a ninety-pound conventional explosive warhead. The Sea Sparrow is guided to its target by a computer-controlled firing system. Two radar transmitters search for and can automatically lock onto an enemy aircraft as far as fifty miles away. The system's computer then calculates the target's coordinates and generates a firing command when the target is within the missile's range (about ten to twelve miles). The automatic firing controls can be overridden and the Sea Sparrow launched manually if the situation calls for it. The *Vinson* has four Sea Sparrow launchers carrying eight missiles, each housed in a boxlike chamber.

The Mark 15 Phalanx is a close-in weapons system (CIWS) that provides "terminal defense" against any enemy aircraft or missile that has penetrated the *Vinson*'s other defensive systems. Two twenty-millimeter rotating Gatling guns make up the firepower element of the CIWS system. These guns can fire up to forty-five hundred rounds per minute continuously or in bursts of sixty or one hundred rounds—a withering fire sure to bring down any hostile plane or missile. Mounted on top of the guns inside a domed enclosure is the Phalanx's firing-control system, containing a search radar for detecting enemy targets and a tracking radar to aim the guns. This system tracks both the enemy target and the outgoing stream of bullets,

The Mark 15 Phalanx fires up to forty-five hundred rounds per minute.

thus enabling the Phalanx to keep locked on even fast-moving missiles.

The USS *Carl Vinson* also carries electronic-warfare systems to detect enemy radar waves, jam the radar of enemy planes and missiles, and launch chaff (small bits of metal foil) or infrared decoys to confuse a radar-guided missile and steer it away from the carrier.

But even with all these onboard weapons a carrier can still be vulnerable to enemy attack, so further protective measures are necessary to ensure the success of a seagoing mission.

Battle Groups of Enduring Freedom

An aircraft carrier is the navy's most important, and most expensive, asset, so it makes sense to provide as much protection as possible for these giant vessels. Carriers do not go into a war zone alone, but are deployed with other ships in a formation known as an aircraft carrier battle group (CVBG). A CVBG—the designation comes from CV, navy shorthand for aircraft carrier, and BG, for battle group—can vary in the number and types of ships deployed for a particular mission. Author Tom Clancy calls the CVBGs "the single most useful military force available in time of crisis or conflict." [10] Since 1979 carrier battle groups have been continuously patrolling the world's waterways, especially in the Mediterranean Sea, the western Pacific Ocean, and the Indian Ocean/Arabian Sea region. The present-day navy has twelve aircraft carriers

and their battle groups ready to respond to a threat anywhere in the world. Five of these CVBGs were deployed for duty in Operation Enduring Freedom. Along with the nuclear-powered carrier USS *Carl Vinson* were the nuclear carriers *Theodore Roosevelt, Enterprise,* and *John C. Stennis,* and the conventionally powered USS *Kitty Hawk.*

A typical battle group will include seven to twelve heavily armed escort ships. In addition to the carrier the CVBG will usually have guided-missile cruisers and destroyers, frigates, attack submarines, and one or more supply ships. In battle group formation, these ships will operate within fifty to one hundred miles from each other, surrounding the carrier with a ring of protection from enemy surface ships, submarines, and aircraft. The outer perimeter, or first line of defense, of this protective ring usually has a radius of some 125 to 150 miles from the aircraft carrier.

Among the ships deployed with the USS *Carl Vinson* battle group during Operation Enduring Freedom was the USS *Princeton,* a guided-missile cruiser commissioned in 1989. At over 560 feet in length, this fast cruiser is powered by four gas turbine engines (similar to the engines in a DC-10 airliner) that can propel it at a speed of more than thirty-four miles per hour. The *Princeton*'s armament includes two Phalanx CIWSs and a variety of missiles.

Guided-missile destroyers are, according to Clancy, "the finest surface combat vessels in the world." [11] The USS *John Paul Jones* is a multimission destroyer that can

A navy technician monitors air traffic aboard an Aegis cruiser.

defend the group against enemy attacks from the air, the ocean surface, or underwater. Armed with surface-to-air and surface-to-surface missiles, as well as torpedoes, deck guns, and the Phalanx CIWS, destroyers such as the *John Paul Jones* are deadly additions to the CVBG.

Modern destroyers and cruisers like the *Princeton* and *John Paul Jones* employ the world's most advanced, fully integrated system for tracking and attacking enemy aircraft, ships, and submarines. The Aegis system consists of several subsystems: a radar system that can simultaneously track up to one hundred airborne and surface targets; a command-and-control system to evaluate targets and assign threat priorities; and a weapons system consisting of various missiles for the actual attack. The Aegis system (named for the protective armor borne by the Greek god Zeus) can also integrate information from other vessels and aircraft.

Prowling silently beneath the waves, two nuclear-powered attack submarines, the USS *Olympia* and the USS *Key West* were also part of the *Carl Vinson* battle group. With the ability to travel at a speed of more than twenty-three miles per hour, these subs carry missiles, torpedoes, and mines designed to destroy both surface and submarine enemies. The *Key West* is equipped with vertical launch tubes in the bow of the vessel. These twelve tubes allow Tomahawk cruise missiles to be fired vertically in rapid succession.

Even though a nuclear-powered aircraft carrier can travel for years without replacing its nuclear fuel, the conventionally powered ships in the battle group will need refueling while under way. In addition, consumables such as food need to be replenished from time to time during an operation. Logistics ships fill this role and are a necessary addition to the battle group. The USS *Sacramento* is a fast combat-support ship that carries a wealth of items needed for the continuous operation of the group: food, aviation fuel for the carrier air wing, spare parts and other supplies, plus ammunition. Two helicopters

stationed aboard the *Sacramento* allow for speedy and efficient vertical replenishment to ships in the battle group. It carries a complete assortment of missiles, bombs, and small ammunition, and can replenish the entire stock of the *Carl Vinson*'s munitions in three to four hours.

"Freedom Versus Evil"

As the USS *Carl Vinson* prepared for its role in Operation Enduring Freedom, Rear Admiral Thomas Zelibor addressed the carrier's crew: "We've been tasked by the President to be ready for combat operations in support of the war on terrorism—freedom versus evil. . . . We've been here a month, ready to operate at a moment's notice. . . . We are the 911 force of choice, and we have a can-do attitude."[12] With that "can-do" attitude, carrier battle groups were assembled in the northern Arabian Sea and the air force was preparing its aircraft on land. The United States was about to take to the skies and deliver the first blows in a conflict that would ultimately topple the Taliban regime and cripple al-Qaeda's terrorist activities.

★ Chapter 2 ★

Air Attack over Afghanistan

The war against terrorism began just twenty-six days after the twin towers of the World Trade Center in New York and the Pentagon just outside Washington were attacked by al-Qaeda terrorists. The terrorists used hijacked commercial airliners as the instruments of their destructive acts. Ironically, the terrorists' base of operations in Afghanistan would ultimately be destroyed by the massive airpower of the United States. Initially, about 150 aircraft were deployed for the opening phases of Operation Enduring Freedom, including land-based air force bombers and refuelers and navy carrier-based aircraft.

Operation Enduring Freedom's initial offensive was an assault on Afghanistan beginning at 9:20 P.M. on October 7, 2001. The mission was to destroy Taliban anti-aircraft artillery and missiles, knock out command-and-control centers, and destroy airfields and as many aircraft on the ground as possible. U.S. intelligence had estimated that the Taliban might have up to thirty Soviet-

made fighters that might pose a threat to U.S. fighters and bombers. But no aircraft were launched in response to the strikes. Thirty-one targets on the ground had been determined by U.S. Central Command, the command in charge of the southwest Asian area of operations. These targets included Kandahār, the center of the Taliban movement; Kabul, Afghanistan's capital city; Jalāl-ābād in eastern Afghanistan; and Mazār-e Sharīf in the north. The initial attacks included twenty-five aircraft from the carriers USS *Carl Vinson* and the USS *Enterprise*.

Aircraft Carrier Operations

The primary purpose of an aircraft carrier is, of course, to bring aircraft into a battle zone or area of international crisis anywhere in the world. The responsibility for carrying out this mission lies with the carrier air wing (CVW), a group of aircraft squadrons attached to a carrier battle group. Although the makeup of a CVW varies depending on the carrier's mission, a typical wing would include three to four squadrons of fighter jets, one airborne early-warning squadron, one electronic-warfare squadron, a squadron for antisubmarine and antisurface warfare, a helicopter squadron, and a logistical-support squadron. Each squadron has its own insignia and unique and colorful nickname. During Operation Enduring Freedom, the air wing assigned to the USS *Carl Vinson* included such squadrons as the "Black-lions," the "Mighty Shrikes," and the "Drag-onfires."

In all, some seventy to eighty-five planes are carried into combat zones, along with fuel and munitions ranging from bombs and missiles to torpedoes and antiship mines. Out of the total complement of some fifty-seven hundred men and women aboard the aircraft carrier, nearly twenty-five hundred are assigned to the air wing. The aircraft carrier, its air wing, its crew, and the companion ships in its battle group make a formidable mobile fighting force.

Flight operations on an aircraft carrier are carried out day or night in any type of weather. Steam-powered catapults can launch thirty-six-ton aircraft from a standstill to 150 miles per hour in three seconds. Landings are made on the angled portion of the carrier's deck, where four steel arresting cables stop a speeding plane in about three hundred feet. Naval and marine aviators have to be expert pilots indeed when it comes to landing an aircraft

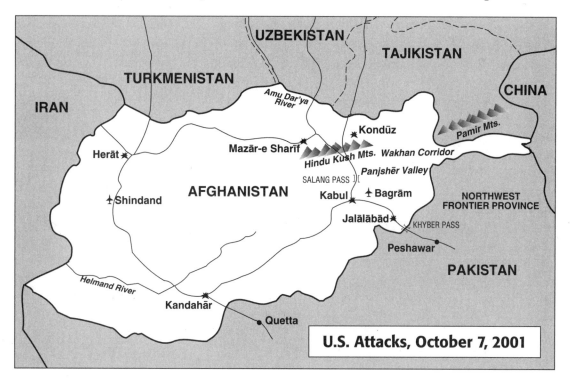

U.S. Attacks, October 7, 2001

at night on a darkened carrier pitching in rough seas.

Among the first aircraft to strike at al-Qaeda and Taliban installations was a plane that had been the navy's premier long-range fighter for thirty years: the supersonic F-14.

Tomcats of the Air

The F-14, popularly known as the Tomcat, was designed by Grumman Aircraft Corporation in the late 1960s to replace aging F-4 Phantoms as the navy's primary fleet defense fighter. The Tomcat made its first test flight in 1970 and entered the fleet in 1973; ultimately more than six hundred F-14s were built. Powered by two turbofan engines, the F-14 carries a crew of two in its tandem cockpit: The pilot occupies the front seat, while the radar intercept officer (RIO) sits in the rear. It is the RIO's job to track enemy targets using a sophisticated radar system and fire the Tomcat's numerous weapons.

Perhaps the most striking feature of the F-14 Tomcat is its wing arrangement. The F-14 is the only navy fighter to employ variable-geometry wings. Depending on the speed of the aircraft and the maneuvers it is carrying out, the Tomcat's wings can swing through an arc of forty-eight degrees. During supersonic flight and dogfights, the

An F-14 Tomcat prepares to launch from the aircraft carrier USS Kitty Hawk.

School for "Top Guns"

The most highly skilled pilots in the U.S. Navy fly carrier jets like the F-14 Tomcat and the F/A-18 Hornet. To train its pilots to become the best of the best, the navy turns to the Naval Strike and Air Warfare Center (NSAWC), popularly known as "Top Gun" since a feature film set at the school made the name well known. Originally designated the Naval Fighter Weapons School, Top Gun was established because of rather discouraging combat results shown by navy fighter pilots during the Vietnam War.

By 1968 naval aviators dogfighting against North Vietnamese pilots in the skies over Southeast Asia had a poor record, downing fewer than three enemy planes for every navy aircraft shot down. At times this ratio even dropped to less than one enemy for every U.S. loss. This was in stark contrast to the navy's World War II record in the Pacific, where fifteen hostile aircraft were destroyed for every U.S. plane lost. Navy captain Frank Ault, a fighter pilot with the Naval Air Systems Command, conducted a study of combat results in Vietnam. In his report Ault suggested that the navy establish a school to teach navy and marine pilots how to use their weapons more effectively in realistic combat situations. In March 1969 the first class of pilots began their training at Miramar Naval Air Station in California and Top Gun was born.

A graduate-level course in aerial combat conducted five times a year, the Top Gun's course teaches pilots advanced techniques in all aspects of combat aviation including tactics, weapons usage, and aerial combat maneuvering. Classroom instruction is accompanied by air combat exercises with Top Gun instructors flying "enemy" planes in realistic dogfight simulations. These exercises, while intense, are merely rehearsals to prepare navy pilots for the real thing that they will have to face in the real world of air combat. The school also holds the Advanced Mission Commander's Course, which teaches airborne battle management and trains air intercept controllers in strike-fighter command and control. In 1996 the school was moved from Miramar to the Naval Air Station at Fallon, Nevada, located about seventy miles from Reno. Today "Top Guns" are still fighting it out over the Nevada desert, preparing for the day when their training may be put to the ultimate test.

wings fold back toward the fuselage, giving the F-14 the streamlined delta shape needed for such demanding flight. When the aircraft is flying slowly the wings swing straight out from the fuselage, giving the pilot better control for carrier takeoffs and landings. The wing sweep is adjusted automatically during flight by the "mach sweep programmer," a computer that calculates the optimum swing for the ever changing speed and attitude of the Tomcat.

Tools for the RIO

While the pilot has the F-14's flight controls in front of him, the radar intercept officer in the rear seat has his own instruments that serve as the information and control center for the Tomcat's weaponry and defense systems. The APG-71 radar unit is an advanced digital radar system that can track multiple targets and has a range of more than two hundred miles. The Joint Tactical Information Distribution System (JTIDS) provides digital communication between the F-14 and ships, ground stations, and other aircraft during tactical combat maneuvers. JTIDS shares information about the location, speed, and identification of enemy aircraft to make targeting more precise and thus result in more effective defense of the carrier battle group. Some F-14s were fitted with a Tactical Airborne Reconnaissance Pod System (TARPS), which carries cameras and infrared sensors for reconnaissance missions. Using TARPS, Tomcats provided images of Afghan terrain and even specific targets for guiding other aircraft in their bombing runs.

Low-Altitude Navigation and Targeting Infrared for Night (LANTIRN) gives the Tomcat the capability of carrying out precision strikes against ground targets day or night in all kinds of weather. With its targeting pod mounted underneath the aircraft, the LANTIRN system uses Forward-Looking Infrared (FLIR) sensors to acquire and lock onto an enemy target. Then lasers guide the F-14's missiles or bombs to the selected target with pinpoint accuracy. Such precision helped Tomcat pilots attack al-Qaeda forces hiding out in the many caves that dot the rugged Afghanistan landscape. But seeking out and destroying al-Qaeda and Taliban strongholds taxed the F-14s and their crews to their limits. "It's a totally different kind of flying,"[13] comments Captain Richard Wren, commanding officer of the USS *Carl Vinson*. Aircraft that normally made two-and-a-half-hour combat sorties flew missions of more than six hours to reach Afghanistan and return to the carrier.

Alongside the F-14 Tomcat another navy strike fighter, the F/A-18 Hornet, also delivered bombs and missiles to targets in Afghanistan.

Stinger in the Sky

As the navy's premier all-weather fighter and attack aircraft, the F/A-18 Hornet made its first test flight in 1978. The F/A designation reflects its capability in air-to-air combat as well as in ground attacks against enemy installations. As a "multirole" aircraft, it served as a replacement for the F-4 Phantom fighter and the A-7 Corsair attack aircraft. Smaller than the F-14 and without the Tomcat's distinctive swing wings, the Hornet is powered by two eighteen-thousand-pound-thrust turbofan engines that give it a top speed of mach 1.7, nearly twice the speed of sound. Depending on the version of the F/A-18, it is operated by a single pilot or, like the Tomcat, a two-person crew.

At the outset, the F/A-18 Hornet was a controversial aircraft due to several design problems and, more seriously, small internal fuel capacity that limited its range and munitions-carrying capability. After these problems were compensated for by a series of design modifications and the use of external fuel tanks, the Hornet entered naval service in 1983. As an attack platform the F/A-18 can externally carry a wide variety of bombs and missiles, almost seven tons of ordnance for both air-to-air and air-to-ground combat. For close-in aerial combat the Hornet relies on a Vulcan twenty-millimeter cannon in the nose of the aircraft. The Vulcan, which is found in both the F/A-18 and F-14, can fire up to six thousand rounds per minute from its six rotating barrels.

It might seem an almost overwhelming task for the F/A-18 pilot to coordinate and

The F/A-18 Hornet (top) carries a Vulcan cannon in the nose of the craft.

the problem by designing a revolutionary new "office" for the Hornet's pilot.

The Glass Cockpit

The cockpit of a modern fighter has literally hundred of gauges, switches, and levers to monitor and control all aspects of the aircraft's operation. But with so much information to digest and decisions to be made, a pilot can quickly become confused. McDonnell Douglas engineers knew they had to create a simplified cockpit for the Hornet. "The trick," recalls designer Eugene C. Adam, "is to do a lot of things automatically for the pilot but never, ever, to leave him in the dark as to what's happening."[14] By replacing dozens of small analog gauges with a few computer screens, relevant information could be instantly displayed and easily seen by the pilot. Because of the large glass surfaces of the screens, the pilot's compartment was soon referred to as the "glass cockpit." Information from the main flight instruments is projected onto a glass screen above the instrument panel. Called a "heads-up display," it allows the pilot to monitor vital flight functions without taking his eyes off the view outside.

Controlling the Hornet was also made easier in the new glass cockpit. With a system called "hands on throttle and stick," buttons and switches to control the F/A-18's weapons are located on the pilot's control stick and throttle. To select between various missiles and the Vulcan gun, the Hornet pilot needs only to flip a switch on the

fire all this weaponry while simultaneously flying the aircraft in difficult combat maneuvers. But engineers at McDonnell Douglas, the manufacturer of the F/A-18, solved

Information from a fighter's "heads-up display" is superimposed on the pilot's field of view.

control stick with his thumb. Other buttons manage the radar system, autopilot, lighting, communications, and additional functions. Attack modes can be instantly changed. "If you're in navigation or air-to-ground mode," says Eugene Adam, "if someone jumps you, you move that switch in any direction and the whole plane reverts to air-to-air."[15]

The glass cockpit represented some of the latest advances in fighter and attack aircraft technology. But even older aircraft found a role in the war against terrorism. The U.S. Air Force filled the skies over Afghanistan with the world's most powerful strategic bomber.

"Big Ugly Fat Fellow"

It saw combat from Vietnam in the 1960s to Operation Desert Storm in the 1990s. It was a major component of the U.S. policy of deterring the spread of communism during the Cold War. It first flew in 1952 and is not scheduled to be phased out until it nears its one hundredth birthday. All these facts are a testimony to the amazing ruggedness and versatility of the B-52 Stratofortress.

When the air force needed a long-range strategic bomber to replace the aging propeller-driven bombers of World War II, the Boeing Aircraft Company came up with the design that eventually became the B-52. After its first successful test flight the Stratofortress entered the air force's arsenal in 1955; in all more than 740 B-52s were manufactured. With eight powerful jet engines tucked under its swept-back wings, the current B-52 can carry a 70,000-pound bomb load at 650 miles per hour to a maximum altitude of 50,000 feet. Its range of 8,800 miles can be extended by in-flight refueling, enabling the B-52 to remain aloft around the clock if the situation warrants. While originally designed to carry nuclear bombs the versatile Stratofortress has performed numerous roles, from delivering conventional munitions and cruise missiles to flying reconnaissance missions and assisting the U.S. Navy in mine-laying operations. It even served as the launch platform for the X-15 rocket plane, a supersonic, high-altitude research aircraft.

The B-52 Stratofortress is operated by a crew of five: the aircraft commander, pilot, navigator, radar navigator, and electronic-warfare officer. With a wingspan of 185 feet and a fuselage length of 160 feet the B-52 dwarfs the newer attack fighters like the F/A-18. Its size and hulking profile has led aviators to give it the nickname "BUFF" (for Big Ugly Fat Fellow). But today's B-52 boasts the latest in electronic-warfare equipment, including an electro-optical viewing system that incorporates FLIR and low-light television cameras. The Global Positioning System and night-vision goggles for the pilots

increase targeting accuracy and collision avoidance.

Flying from Diego Garcia

In addition to carrier-based air strikes on Afghanistan, B-52 bomber sorties originated from the island of Diego Garcia in the middle of the Indian Ocean. As a part of the British Indian Ocean Territory, Diego Garcia is ruled by the United Kingdom, America's staunchest ally in peace and at war. But for the past thirty years, Diego Garcia has been inhabited mostly by U.S. military personnel. During the Cold War the island (actually a coral atoll) served as a naval and air support facility, and was used as a refueling base in the Persian Gulf War. According to Mark Thompson, a correspondent for *Time* magazine, "As a long-range base, Diego is perfect. It's convenient, it's isolated and you don't have to deal with recalcitrant allies or terrorist attacks. It's an immovable aircraft carrier."[16]

Unlike seagoing carriers, however, this "immovable aircraft carrier" has a twelve-thousand-foot runway to accommodate the huge B-52. Air force ground crews worked around the clock to maintain the aircraft and load them with munitions in preparation for the next round of bomb runs. With Diego Garcia some twenty-nine hundred miles from Afghanistan, round-trip flights to the target zone and back to the island took more than twelve hours. Once over Afghanistan, pilots were always mindful of the possibility of antiaircraft fire. But early strikes on ground installations effectively suppressed the Taliban's defensive capabilities. "The air defenses we've seen have been minimal," commented one pilot, adding, however, that "you're definitely looking [for threats] the whole time you're there." [17] Tensions for the crew ease a bit once the bombs have been delivered and they are heading home. "You're more relaxed, in a sense," said a flight crew member. "But at the same time, our feet aren't on the ground, and we still have a lot more flying to do." [18]

While flying for twelve to fifteen hours may be no picnic for the B-52 crews, it is a short trip compared to the hours logged by pilots in the air force's B-2 stealth bombers.

The "Invisible" Bomber

Among the aircraft engaged in the war on terrorism were B-2 Spirit stealth bombers. During the first five days of Operation Enduring Freedom, B-2 Spirit bombers made nonstop flights from their home at Whiteman Air Force Base in Missouri to Afghanistan—exhausting combat sorties that lasted more than forty hours, including a record-breaking forty-four-hour flight.

Dark gray in color, batlike, and angular, the B-2 looks unlike any other aircraft

The B-52 Stratofortress flew bombing runs on Afghanistan from the long-range base Diego Garcia.

New Ways of Bombing

One of the results of the air war on Afghanistan was the development of new methods of using bombers and attack aircraft in combat situations. Modern bombing techniques used in Operation Enduring Freedom have helped to minimize incomplete missions and wasted munitions caused by poor weather, navigational difficulties, or faulty intelligence. One of those techniques is flex-targeting. "Flex targeting is the ability to change targets while en route," explains air force major Andy Thompson in an article by Timothy Hoffman, "Air Force Bomber Tactics . . . ," posted on the official U.S. Air Force website (www.af.mil): "Many times bombers start their mission eight hours or more from their target. A lot can happen in a combat theater in eight hours. . . . The crews can receive new target information while they are in the air and then go on and hit the new targets." The success of this strategy is demonstrated by the fact that 80 percent of the targets hit during Operation Enduring Freedom were flex targets.

The extensive use of aerial refueling during the war was also a part of the flex-targeting strategy. As Rear Admiral John Stufflebeem, deputy director of the Joint Staff, explained during a press conference (www.defenselink.mil): "We're using power in ways today that we had never thought [of] before. For instance, bombers that go to a target, come back to a tanker, and are sent to another target. That's flex-targeting. That's using bombers in a way that we hadn't previously done . . . flexibility that this environment breeds."

Once the initial bombing of Afghanistan had taken out the antiaircraft capability of the Taliban, coalition pilots could seek targets within areas known as "engagement zones." An engagement zone (sometimes called a "kill box") is a geographic area on the ground within which pilots are assigned certain types of targets to attack. For example, a pilot's mission may be to go after radar installations, tanks, or mobile missile launchers in a particular engagement zone. A controller in the air will find those targets and relay their locations to the bomber pilot who will then proceed to attack and destroy them. During such operations "targets of opportunity" may show up, such as a tank or truck that the pilot discovers. After receiving positive identification of the hostile target from the controller, the pilot is given the go-ahead to attack.

in the skies. The unique appearance of the B-2 Spirit is reminiscent of the YB-49 "Flying Wing," a tailless post–World War II bomber that never went into production. The B-2 was first flown in 1989 and became operational in 1993. Its 172-foot swept wing flows smoothly into the fuselage; no vertical or horizontal tailplanes are needed because sophisticated computers control the aircraft's stability. The Spirit is powered by four turbofan engines, located deep inside the wing, that give it an unrefueled range of nearly seven thousand miles and a top altitude of fifty thousand feet. It has a crew of two (three fewer than the B-52) and can carry forty thousand pounds of munitions ranging from conventional and precision-guided bombs to nuclear weapons. But the most unique aspect of the B-2's design is stealth qualities. "The B-2's low-observable, or 'stealth,' characteristics," comments air force major J.C. Valle, "give it the unique ability to penetrate an enemy's most sophisticated defenses and threaten its most valued, and heavily defended, targets."[19]

The aircraft's profile is sleek, appearing from the front to be more like a fighter than a heavy bomber. This very low "radar cross section" (RCS) minimizes the radar return signal the B-2 will generate on enemy radar screens. Measured in square meters, an aircraft's RCS should be as close to zero as possible. The B-2 has an RCS of only .06 square meters; in comparison, the RCS of a B-52 is about sixty square meters. In practical terms, the B-2 looks no bigger than a bird on a radar screen. The composite material (a plasticlike carbon fiber) used to build the B-2 and its dark gray finish are also important for stealth operations, absorbing radar waves rather than reflecting them, thus further minimizing returns. The engine intakes of the B-2 are designed to minimize noise, and the jet exhaust is cooled and routed through an exhaust trench at the wing's trailing edge to minimize the heat signature that could be picked up by infrared sensors.

The Spirit's large bomb-load capacity made the aircraft valuable in destroying Taliban radar installations, military headquarters, and other targets in the opening days of the war. After dropping their munitions on Afghanistan, the B-2s headed for Diego Garcia, briefly landing on the island for an "engine running" crew change. Then they were airborne once more and heading home, another thirty hours in the air for the new crew.

The Supersonic Lancer

Combine the sleek wing/body contours of a B-2, the variable wing geometry of an F-14, and the range and munitions capacity of a B-52, and you have the B-1B Lancer, a strategic bomber for the twenty-first century. Based at Diego Garcia along with the B-52 Stratofortresses, the B-1B played an important role in Operation Enduring Freedom. But the Lancer almost did not get built.

Originally developed during the 1970s, the B-1 program was canceled in 1977 due to budget concerns. President Ronald Reagan revived the program in 1981 and the bomber, now known as the B-1B, became operational in 1986. Ultimately, the Lancer will replace the B-52 as it nears the end of its operational lifetime. This needle-nosed supersonic bomber can carry up to seventy-five thousand pounds of munitions on unrefueled intercontinental missions. Although it has an operational ceiling of about thirty thousand feet, the B-1B's swing-wing design and terrain-following electronics allow for ultralow-level bomb runs that permit precision targeting and make detection by the enemy difficult. Three weapon bays can be configured to carry a variety of conventional and nuclear weapons. Like the B-2 Spirit, the B-1B has a low radar cross section and a radar-absorbing coating that help avoid detection by enemy radar. The Lancer also employs electronic jamming equipment to jam hostile radar signals and can launch chaff, or decoy flares, to further confuse enemy radar-guided missiles.

Its huge payload capacity and the ability to mount various types of weapons, depending on the goals of a mission, made the B-1B one of the primary land-based

bombers in the war on terrorism. The swift and devastating success of their missions soon ushered in a new phase in the war.

The B-1B Lancer can carry many different types of weapons and is difficult to detect by radar.

Spectre and Spooky

After the first week of high-altitude attacks by strategic bombers, carrier-based strike aircraft, and missiles, the Taliban's major air defenses had been suppressed and much of its military capability destroyed. While the strategic bombardment continued, other types of aircraft entered the war to seek out and destroy "targets of opportunity." On October 15, 2001, AC-130 aircraft made their first sorties over Afghanistan. Known by the call signs "Spectre" or "Spooky," the AC-130

is truly an airborne gunship in every sense of the word.

First used in the Vietnam War, the AC-130 originated as a C-130 cargo plane modified to carry not cargo, but heavy weaponry. With a wingspan of 132 feet and a tail height of 38 feet, the AC-130 and its crew of thirteen or fourteen flies at a leisurely three hundred miles per hour. But the huge turboprop aircraft packs a wallop: The latest "Spooky" version has a 40 mm cannon, a 105 mm howitzer, and a rapid-firing six-barrel Gatling gun. These weapons can pour

Deadly Warthog

Its official designation is the A-10 Thunderbolt, but just one look at this ungainly aircraft will make it clear why it has earned the nickname "Warthog." While it is not as sleek as an F-14 nor as awe inspiring as a B-52, the A-10 is a rugged fighting machine that can sustain an enormous amount of battle damage and still bring its pilot home safely.

Designed to provide close air support for ground forces, the A-10 is powered by twin turbofan engines mounted on the rear fuselage. It has a top speed of over four hundred miles per hour and a ceiling of some forty-five thousand feet, but the Warthog can also "loiter" over a battlefield and operate lower than one thousand feet. Its armament includes a 30 mm seven-barrel Gatling gun and up to sixteen thousand pounds of bombs and missiles carried under its wings and fuselage. The A-10 can take off and land on short airstrips, and its simple design makes for easy servicing at forward areas where repair facilities are limited.

But its ruggedness is what endears the Warthog to its pilots. It can take a hit from armor-piercing shells and keep on flying. Fuel tanks are foam-lined and self-sealing, and the flight control system includes manual backups so the A-10 can be controlled even with its hydraulic system damaged. A "bathtub" of titanium armor protects the entire cockpit. As aircraft go the A-10 may be called homely, even downright ugly. But to its pilots and the ground troops it protects, the Warthog is a beautiful machine.

out a tremendous volley of shells as the aircraft flies in a low circular orbit, banked so that the gun barrels protruding from the left side of the plane can aim at the selected targets. Its firing-control computers, infrared sensors, and all-light-level TV system allow pinpoint accuracy of ground targets. So fierce is the gunship's firepower that it can completely fill an area the size of a football field with shells in mere seconds.

The AC-130 proved ideal for the new phase of the war in Afghanistan. "The AC-130 gunship is an excellent platform to use in this environment," comments General Gregory S. Newbold. "It has precision weapons platforms that allow us to reduce collateral damage at the impact point. It is a system with a long loiter capability so it has the ability to station itself over a target area for a long period of target-time."[20] In addition to attacking such targets as Taliban troop concentrations, vehicles, and weapons storage sites, the AC-130 has a psychological effect. Just the sound of Spooky's four turboprop engines can strike terror in the hearts of enemy troops. "They circle the target," says General Wesley Clark, a former NATO commander. "They make a fierce noise. And they just obliterate everything. . . . They are one of the most terrifying things imaginable if you are underneath them."[21]

Underneath a Spooky gunship, or anywhere on the ground in Afghanistan during Operation Enduring Freedom for that matter, was not a safe place for the Taliban to be. The bombs dropped by U.S. aircraft in the war on terrorism included some of the most sophisticated and effective munitions developed by modern military science. And, as the Taliban soon found out, they were also quite deadly.

Chapter 3

Bombs and Missiles

Dropping bombs on an adversary from the air has been a part of warfare since World War I, when pilots of rickety biplanes tossed grenades out of the cockpit onto enemy lines below. World War II, a conflict that witnessed devastating strategic bombing, was ended by two atomic bombs dropped on Japan. In the Vietnam War, carpet bombing laid waste to vast areas of the country's terrain in Operation Rolling Thunder. Airpower proved itself once more in the war in Afghanistan as U.S. and coalition aircraft destroyed the Taliban's military capability with aerial bombardment. Among the munitions used was a wide variety of bombs, both "dumb" and "smart," and missiles that could seek out and hit their targets with astonishing accuracy.

Dropping Iron

For most of the twentieth century, bombs were relatively simple devices. In basic terms, a bomb is an amount of explosive material encased in a metal shell. Additionally, a bomb will usually have tail fins to stabilize it as it falls, and a fuse to detonate the explosive at the proper time. Beyond these basics, however, the variety of shapes, sizes, and types of explosive is almost limitless. Bombs are divided into several classes according to the job they are required to do: general purpose, cluster, penetration, and fragmentation. Referred to as iron, free-fall, or "dumb" bombs (so-called because they have no active guidance system), conventional munitions are the simplest way for aircraft to deliver explosives to ground targets.

The first objective of Operation Enduring Freedom was to destroy Taliban command centers, antiaircraft installations, and air bases, and thus disrupt the enemy's ability to fight back. In the first week of the operation some two thousand bombs were delivered to ground targets in Afghanistan by land- and carrier-based aircraft. Of the munitions dropped, about one thousand were Mk 82 bombs, one of the most common types of bombs.

Navy airmen remove a stabilizing unit from an Mk 82 bomb.

A member of the Mark 80 (usually referred to by abbreviation Mk 80) series of munitions originally developed in the 1950s, the Mk 82 is a cylindrical free-fall munition five and one-half feet long and nearly eleven inches in diameter. It weighs five hundred pounds, about 40 percent of which is its high explosive payload. Four fins stabilize the bomb during its descent and keep its nose down for proper detonation. Different types of fuses, located in either the nose or tail (or sometimes both), can be mounted in the Mk 82 depending on the type of results desired from the explosion. An impact fuse detonates the bomb on impact and is useful against such targets as airfield runways or supply depots. Proximity fuses use radar to trigger the explosion just before impact with the ground, to destroy military vehicles, troops, and other aboveground targets vulnerable to shrapnel. Time-delayed fuses are often used against enemy buildings, allowing the bomb to penetrate the structure before exploding.

In the opening phase of Operation Enduring Freedom, all land-based bombers and carrier-based fighters were capable of carrying the Mk 82. Those used on carrier aircraft were "thermally protected" to reduce the chance of an accidental explosion should there be a jet-fuel fire on board the carrier. Along with the Mk 82, other bombs in the Mk 80 series include the Mk 83 one-thousand-pound and Mk 84 two-thousand-pound bombs. Simplicity, reliability, and relatively low cost (an Mk 82 costs only about three hundred dollars) are all advantages of using dumb bombs. More complicated, and therefore more devastating, than the simple Mk 82 are the specialized dumb bombs known as cluster munitions.

Cluster Bombs

The cluster bomb unit, or CBU, is a weapons system that can be configured for specific missions or general-purpose military objectives. These versatile munitions have been used by U.S. forces since the war in Vietnam. The key to the operation of a cluster bomb is a load of smaller explosive devices carried within the bomb casing. The CBU submunitions, or "bomblets," vary in size, shape, and number depending on the target to be destroyed. Cluster bombs can hold anywhere from 40 to more than 650 bomblets and, like the Mk 82, are unguided

Cluster Bombs: Enticing Dangers

Although cluster munitions can be highly effective in war, they often leave a dangerous legacy long after the fighting is over. Since the beginning of the air strikes on October 7, 2001, it is estimated that more than twelve hundred cluster bombs were dropped on Afghanistan during Operation Enduring Freedom. Each bomb carried about two hundred submunitions, resulting in nearly a quarter of a million bomblets landing on Afghan soil. When they work as designed, these bomblets can be devastating against enemy vehicles and troops. But not all bomblets will explode, and therein lies the problem.

The manufacturers of cluster bombs and the U.S. military report that the bomblets have a failure rate of about 5 to 7 percent. This figure would indicate that more than twelve thousand unexploded bomblets remained after the properly working ones had detonated. But many human rights organizations dispute these numbers. They claim that the failure rate is closer to 20 or 30 percent, meaning that more than seventy-five thousand duds are waiting to be set off by unsuspecting civilians. Unfortunately, many innocent victims of unexploded cluster bombs are children.

The color of cluster submunitions is one reason why the unexploded bomblets are so dangerous. About the size and shape of a soda can, the bright yellow bomblets are attractive to a child or other person who is unaware of the danger they pose. Additionally, a yellow bomblet is approximately the same color as the more than 2 million humanitarian daily rations (HDRs) dropped over Afghanistan to feed starving refugees. Someone who thinks he or she is retrieving a food packet may actually be reaching for a cluster bomblet instead, with lethal results.

U.S. radio broadcasts warned Afghan citizens against mistaking the cylindrical bomblets for the rectangular HDRs, and plans were made to change the color of the food packages. Under the auspices of the United Nations, demining teams are working to rid Afghanistan of dud cluster munitions, mines, and other unexploded ordnance. But as one of the most embattled nations on Earth, Afghanistan has more than 10 million unexploded munitions still waiting to be defused.

munitions that rely on gravity to carry them to their targets.

The submunitions themselves—officially designated by the prefix BLU for bomb live unit—can be round, cylindrical, or pointed like darts. Some bomblets are designed to be effective against "soft targets," that is, nonarmored vehicles such as trucks or enemy personnel. According to Rear Admiral John Stufflebeem, deputy director of operations of the Joint Chiefs of Staff, "cluster munitions are most effective against troops that are in lightly defended positions. So the best place to use them is in an area that would have minimal collateral damage impact and maximum numbers of forces that you would wish to kill." [22] Other BLUs are designed to destroy heavily armored vehicles such as tanks and personnel carriers. Variously timed fuses can cause the submunitions to detonate aboveground, upon hitting the ground, or at random intervals after impact. The BLUs create blast effects, fragmentation damage, and incendiary, or fire-producing, effects. One type of cluster bomb, called a fuel/air explosive unit, disperses a mist of highly flammable fuel some sixty feet in diameter over its target. When a detonator ignites the fuel thirty feet above the ground a huge explosion occurs, which can clear minefields, destroy armored vehicles and parked aircraft, and annihilate troop concentrations.

Although hundreds of bomblets are dispersed from a typical cluster bomb, not all the submunitions will explode. This has made the CBU a controversial weapons system. Unexploded bomblets can be dangerous to local civilians, especially to curious children. Despite the controversy, however, Secretary of Defense Donald Rumsfeld made it clear why cluster bombs were necessary in the war on terrorism: "They are being used on front-line al-Qaeda and Taliban troops to try to kill them, is why we're using them, to be perfectly blunt." [23]

The CBU-87

By December 1, 2001, U.S. bombers had dropped, along with other types of munitions, some six hundred cluster bombs on Afghanistan. Among those was the CBU-87, a thousand-pound "combined effects munition" that measures 7.5 feet tall and 15 inches in diameter. The CBU-87 is a dumb bomb, propelled only by gravity and guided by a set of tail fins, and it can be carried by most attack and bomber aircraft in the air force and navy arsenals. The body of this bomb is actually a dispenser containing 202 submunitions designated BLU-97. These cylindrical bomblets measure approximately 7.75 inches long and 2.25 inches wide. At a predetermined altitude the CBU-87 spins and opens to disperse its submunitions over a wide area—sometimes as large as several football fields. Each cylindrical bomblet is slowed and stabilized by an inflatable parachutelike decelerator that, when deployed, also arms the bomblet. When they explode, the bomblets spread fragments in all directions and can also start

The BLU-82, or Daisy Cutter, is the largest nonnuclear bomb.

fires with a flammable zirconium ring. The explosive load of each submunition is a "shaped charge" capable of penetrating 5 inches of armor plating if detonated on contact with a tank or other armored vehicle.

While cluster bombs are versatile and effective weapons, nothing in the military arsenal of any nation can match the raw power of the BLU-82—the world's largest bomb.

The "Daisy Cutter"

It weighs fifteen thousand pounds and is the size of a small car. Too heavy for ordinary bombers or attack aircraft, it must be dropped from a cargo plane. And although it is only one-thousandth as powerful as the first atomic bomb dropped on Hiroshima, Japan, at the end of World War II, its power is awesome.

The BLU-82 is the largest conventional (nonnuclear) bomb in existence. It was first used in 1970 during the Vietnam War to clear large areas of dense jungle for helicopter landing zones. Known as Commando Vault in Vietnam, it was called the Daisy Cutter in the Persian Gulf War, where eleven BLU-82s were dropped on Iraqi targets. In that war, as well as in the war on terrorism, the Daisy Cutter was deployed as an antipersonnel weapon creating both devastating blast damage and psychological effects against the enemy. The cylindrical bomb measures almost twelve feet long and four and a half feet in diameter. Inside its quarter-inch-steel body is 12,600 pounds of an explosive slurry, a watery mixture of ammonium nitrate and aluminum powder that creates a powerful blast upon detonation. Projecting from the Daisy Cutter's tapered nose is a fuse extender that triggers the bomb to explode about three feet above the ground.

To deliver the BLU-82 to its target the bomb is mounted on a sledlike cradle and then loaded into an MC-130 Combat Talon aircraft, a version of the huge plane that also operates as the AC-130 gunship. Flying at a minimum of six thousand feet over the target, the MC-130's rear cargo door is opened and a parachute extracts the bomb from the cargo bay. Slowed and stabilized by the parachute during its fall, the Daisy Cutter detonates when its fuse extension hits the ground, resulting in an explosion that causes destruction above ground level but leaves little or no crater. The blast of a Daisy Cutter is distinctive, unlike that of smaller bombs. David Williams, a British journalist in Afghanistan, describes a Daisy Cutter explosion he had witnessed:

Each of the previous explosions (of smaller bombs) . . . had been similar in sight and sound. But then a single aircraft, a C-130 cargo plane flying at about 6,000 feet, could be seen against the brilliant blue sky as it approached Kalakata, where foreign fighters from Osama bin Laden's al-Qaeda network—Pakistanis, Arabs, and Chechens—are based. It was the only warning that a different bomb was to be used.

As the plane banked away . . . there was an explosion far bigger, far deeper and far more sinister than anything I had heard so far in the U.S. bombing campaign. The sound split the air. It was like a thunderclap directly overhead at the height of a ferocious storm. I could see the massive oily black cloud of the explosion as it rolled across the hillside, a mixture of thick smoke, chunks of earth and debris. [24]

The psychological effect of such a powerful blast on enemy troops is also a part of the Daisy Cutter's effectiveness. In one instance during the Gulf War, the entire staff of an Iraqi battalion surrendered after seeing a Daisy Cutter explode nearby. According to journalist Williams, the Daisy Cutter was used in Afghanistan "to take out as many Taliban soldiers as possible with one strike, and to put huge psychological fear into the survivors, making them dread further attacks." [25]

While dumb bombs are undeniably effective, one of the main drawbacks of ordinary munitions is their accuracy, or lack of it. Lower accuracy means fewer hits on target and the possibility of unwanted civilian casualties. For more precise targeting of Taliban installations and troops in Afghanistan, the U.S. military used bombs that were smarter than their ordinary "dumb" cousins.

Precision-Guided Munitions

Precision-guided munitions, also known as smart weapons, utilize various forms of guidance systems to direct them to their targets with far greater accuracy than is possible with standard bombs. Smart bombs are so precise that "a single strike airplane carrying two 'smart' bombs could function as effectively as 108 World War II B-17 bombers carrying 648 bombs and crewed by 1,080 airmen."[26] Television, infrared sensors, lasers, and Global Positioning System receivers are all used to guide smart bombs. Some smart bombs are designed with guidance systems in them, while others are made smart by modifying dumb bombs. In this latter cate-

gory is one of the key weapons used in the war on terrorism in Afghanistan: the JDAM, or Joint Direct-Attack Munition.

The JDAM was used from the beginning of Operation Enduring Freedom. In the first five days alone five hundred JDAMs were dropped on Taliban positions; throughout the operation some sixty-seven hundred were delivered out of a total of twenty-two thousand bombs dropped on Afghanistan. The JDAM is essentially a guidance kit that is added to an existing dumb bomb, such as the one-thousand-pound Mk 83 or two-thousand-pound Mk 84. The modified Mk 83 is designated GBU-31 (for Guided Bomb Unit) and the Mk 84 version is called the GBU-32. All of the bomber and strike aircraft used in Operation Enduring Freedom were capable of carrying JDAMs.

The Taliban Stinger

In the war on terrorism, the weapons used by the Taliban were no match for the forces of Operation Enduring Freedom. But one weapon that did concern U.S. forces was a small, shoulder-mounted missile known as the Stinger. Ironically, the Taliban acquired these missiles not in a clandestine arms deal but from the United States.

The Stinger is a "man-portable" surface-to-air missile designed to shoot down low-flying enemy aircraft. Weighing about thirty-five pounds, the Stinger is fired from a shoulder-mounted launcher and can reach a maximum altitude of ten thousand feet. Its high explosive warhead is directed to the target by infrared sensors that lock onto an aircraft engine's hot exhaust.

In 1986 the United States gave Afghan rebels nearly one thousand Stinger missiles to fight So-

viet forces that had invaded Afghanistan in 1979. The missiles proved extremely effective against Soviet helicopters. After the Soviets left Afghanistan and the Taliban took over, the remaining Stingers fell into their hands. U.S. efforts to buy back the missiles met with little success, and several hundred Stingers remained in the Taliban's possession.

Many experts discounted the Stinger threat during the war in Afghanistan, saying that the batteries used to operate the missiles would have been long since dead. However, others suggested a new, even more ominous scenario involving this weapon: the possibility that a terrorist might use a Stinger to shoot down a U.S. commercial airliner. After September 11, such a scheme seems all too plausible.

The JDAM modification kit includes a Global Positioning System (GPS) receiver, an inertial guidance system, and a set of aluminum tail fins. Each kit costs the U.S. military twenty-one thousand dollars and can be added to a bomb in minutes with just hand tools. Once the JDAM is fitted into a bomber's bomb bay or attached under a strike fighter's wing, target coordinates are loaded to the JDAM's computer system from the host aircraft. When the aircraft reaches its release point, which can be up to fifteen miles from the target, the JDAM is released in level flight or "lofted" as the aircraft climbs. Signals from GPS satellites tell the JDAM where it is at all times as well as pinpoint the position of its target. This information is used by the JDAM's inertial guidance system to position the tail fins, steering the bomb to the target. JDAMs are extremely accurate: Half of all JDAMs impact within forty-three feet of their targets. Even

if the GPS signals are lost due to weather or enemy jamming, the bomb still usually lands within one hundred feet of the target. "It will go miles in any direction," says air force general Leroy Barnidge Jr. "It will hit the targets you can pick out with radar, or it can hit targets you can't see but you know their exact location." [27]

Caves and Bunkers

The success of Operation Enduring Freedom's air campaign soon drove the Taliban into hiding underground. Thousands of limestone caves formed by naturally flowing water lie beneath the mountains of Afghanistan. In addition, more than two thousand years ago Afghan farmers began building a network of shafts and irrigation trenches called *karez* throughout the mountains to

Crew members load an Mk 86 JDAM bomb onto an F/A-18 Hornet fighter.

Bunker Buster bombs can penetrate up to twenty feet of concrete.

bring water to their fields. During the war with the Soviet Union in the 1980s Afghan rebels began expanding these natural caverns and irrigation trenches, turning them into reinforced bunkers large enough to hide men and military equipment. After the Soviets left in defeat in 1989, terrorist leader Osama bin Laden spent millions of dollars to expand and further fortify these underground outposts. The largest bunkers are several stories tall, reinforced with concrete, and protected by steel doors. Numerous escape routes have been hewn out of the rock, and minefields defend the entrances from invading forces. Inside the bunkers are areas for storing fuel, ammunition, and weapons, as well as living and sleeping quarters for al-Qaeda troops. During the Soviet invasion Afghan rebel soldiers could hide in relative safety in the bunkers. "Even if they bombed us," says a former rebel fighter, "we wouldn't even know it because we were down so deep. We weren't even afraid of an atom bomb."[28]

But U.S. forces would not need an atom bomb to attack bunkers where al-Qaeda and Taliban troops were hiding. They had a smart bomb designed especially for the job.

Busting Bunkers

The entrances of the Afghan mountain hideouts were designed with a right-angle turn to prevent missiles from entering the bunkers. But the GBU-28 does not need an entrance to do its work; it makes its own opening in "hardened," or reinforced, targets. Called the Bunker Buster, the GBU-28 is a five-thousand-pound bomb carrying a BLU-113 "Penetrator" warhead filled with nearly 650 pounds of Tritonol, a high explosive. First used in 1991 in the Persian Gulf War, the Bunker Buster is long and thin, its warhead originally built from surplus eight-inch army artillery tubes. After that conflict (in which two Bunker Busters were dropped) the GBU-28 was redesigned, giving it its current length of nineteen feet and diameter of fourteen and a half inches. Fins at the front and rear of the bomb stabilize it in flight, and a clear nose dome covers a sophisticated guidance system.

The Bunker Buster is guided to its target by the use of lasers. When a target is located, it is illuminated by a laser from either ground troops or an aircraft flying above the battlefield. When the GBU-28 is dropped from an attack aircraft such as the air force's F-15 Eagle or B-2 stealth bomber, sensors in the bomb's nose lock onto the laser energy that is reflected from the target. The slim shape of the GBU-28 is a key to its effectiveness. "If you have a pencil," explains an air force official, "its shape makes it easier to penetrate a substance than a baseball bat or broom handle."[29] The Bunker Buster can penetrate up to twenty feet of concrete before the warhead explodes, destroying the interior of its target, whether that is an enemy building or an underground bunker.

Another penetrating weapon used in Afghanistan was the thermobaric type of bomb. After blasting through the outer walls of the bunker a thermobaric bomb creates a deadly explosive cloud that spreads throughout the bunker, displacing all the oxygen inside. According to retired air force general Don Shepperd, a thermobaric bomb will "kill the people that are in there, but won't collapse the cave. Then you can go in and find out what's in there."[30]

All bombs, whether dumb or smart, must ultimately rely on gravity to carry them to their targets. Missiles, on the other hand, can propel themselves to a waiting target, sometimes even before the enemy knows they are coming.

Deadly Tomahawk

From the beginning of the war on terrorism the Tomahawk missile has been an integral part of Operation Enduring Freedom. In fact, Tomahawks were part of the opening bombardment on October 7, 2001, when some fifty of the missiles were fired into Afghanistan from U.S. and British vessels in the Arabian Sea. The Tomahawk land attack missile is an all-weather cruise missile that can be launched from a surface vessel or a submarine. Another version of the Tomahawk is used for antiship operations. At just over eighteen feet long and having a wingspan of nearly nine feet, the Tomahawk can carry a one-thousand-pound conventional warhead or 166 bomblets in a cluster munitions dispenser. It is a subsonic missile with a maximum speed of 550 miles per hour and a range of about one thousand miles. But what makes the Tomahawk a highly "survivable" weapon is its ability to fly low, at about one hundred to three hundred feet, and quickly maneuver to avoid detection by enemy radar.

Boosted from its launcher by a solid-fuel rocket engine, the Tomahawk begins the cruise phase of its flight when a turbofan engine takes over. Using terrain-contour-matching radar, the missile matches its internal digital maps to the actual terrain below its flight path to guide it toward its target. As the Tomahawk nears its destination an optical system, the digital scene-matching area correlation, compares a preloaded image of the target with the actual target and guides the missile to its final strike. Global Positioning System receivers in newer Tomahawks make

locating and hitting enemy targets even more accurate.

The U.S. warships *Philippine Sea, John Paul Jones, O'Brien,* and *McFaul* all launched Tomahawks on the first day of the attacks, as did a U.S. and two British submarines. An F-14 pilot from the aircraft carrier USS *Carl*

The New Missile Threat

During the Cold War, the ideological conflict between the United States and the Soviet Union that raged for decades after World War II, the most feared, and fearsome, weapon was the intercontinental ballistic missile (ICBM). Able to deliver a nuclear warhead thousands of miles, the ICBM threat dominated international relations until the collapse of the Soviet Union in 1991. In the war on terrorism another type of missile helped to defeat the Taliban: the cruise missile.

A cruise missile is basically a pilotless flying bomb that can carry a variety of warheads, including nuclear munitions. Unlike the ICBM, which travels in a ballistic trajectory that takes it to the edge of space, a cruise missile flies more like an airplane, using wings to provide lift and cruising at low altitude to reach its target. Cruise missiles can be launched from aircraft, ships, or submarines, making them ideal for a regional conflict such as Operation Enduring Freedom.

The idea of an unmanned "flying bomb" originated in France before World War I, and soon the United States and Germany began developing their own designs. The U.S. *Sperry Aerial Torpedo* of 1918 was an unmanned biplane loaded with TNT and launched toward the enemy. At a predetermined time the engine shut itself off and the plane would dive toward its target. Although the war ended before the *Aerial Torpedo* could be used, test flights proved that an unmanned aerial weapon was feasible. Experiments continued and by World War II Germany had developed the V-1 "buzz bomb." Powered by a pulse-jet engine and loaded with high explosives, the V-1 was guided to its tar-

get by a gyroscope and compass system. About ten thousand V-1s were launched against Britain from June 1944 to March 1945, causing more than forty-five thousand casualties in London and its suburbs.

During the 1950s the United States developed a number of cruise missiles bearing such names as Matador, Regulus, Navaho, and Snark. But recurring guidance problems and the growing arsenals of the newer ICBMs put an end to cruise missile development. Then in the 1970s, with arms treaties limiting ICBM stockpiles, the United States began to take another look at cruise missiles. Breakthroughs in microelectronics meant smaller and more reliable guidance systems, while improved jet engines and sophisticated terrain-following systems made the cruise missile a formidable weapon. The Persian Gulf War of 1991 saw the first operational use of Tomahawk cruise missiles, with nearly three hundred Tomahawks launched during the conflict. In the opening days of Operation Enduring Freedom, Tomahawks fired from U.S. and British surface ships and submarines destroyed vital Taliban and al-Qaeda facilities in Afghanistan.

Cruise missiles have become an integral part of modern warfare. Because they are simple in design and inexpensive, they can be built or bought by almost any moderately industrialized country. More than seventy nations now include cruise missiles in their arsenals. But what is more disturbing is the fact that they are ideal vehicles for carrying biological and chemical warfare agents. Such capabilities make the cruise missile truly as fearsome a weapon as the Cold War's ICBMs.

Vinson describes the Tomahawk attack as seen from high in the sky: "We'd look down and see [Tomahawk] explosions everywhere, and as soon as those explosions started, that's when the surface fire started coming up."[31] The next day fifteen more Tomahawks were launched; throughout the first two months of the war as many as one hundred Tomahawks were fired into Afghanistan. At a price of about $1 million apiece, attacking with Tomahawks is not cheap. But their accuracy and ability to avoid radar detection made them a valuable weapon in Operation Enduring Freedom.

Maverick

At one point in the war on terrorism a group of al-Qaeda troops had hidden themselves under a bridge near Kabul. A U.S. ground soldier radioed to a Navy F/A-18 pilot, "Hey, we don't want you to blow up the

Technicians inspect AGM-65 Maverick missiles on the flight deck of the USS Enterprise.

bridge, but there are about 50 of the enemy hiding underneath. We want you to put ordnance [a bomb or missile] under the bridge."[32] The pilot placed a missile precisely under the bridge, killing many of the enemy without destroying the bridge. The missile was an AGM-65 Maverick laser-guided weapon.

A tactical air-to-surface missile, the Maverick is eight feet long and one foot in diameter. A wingspan of two feet, four inches allows the Maverick to fly more than seventeen miles under the power of a solid-fuel rocket. Capable of being launched from air force, navy, and marine strike aircraft, the Maverick can carry up to a three-hundred-pound warhead that is detonated either by contact or delayed to penetrate armored vehicles and other hardened targets. Different models of the Maverick can employ either television, infrared, or laser guidance systems to direct them precisely to their targets.

In the war on terrorism, new weapons mix with old traditions from wars past. One of those traditions is the writing of messages on ordnance to be delivered to the enemy. On an air force Maverick missile destined to be carried over Afghanistan, someone wrote a brief but solemn reminder of the reason for all the bombs, missiles, and military personnel deployed half a world away: "In memory of 9-11-2001."

Chapter 4

Support Aircraft and Helicopters

During Operation Enduring Freedom, aircraft conducted a total of 55,150 sorties, or individual missions flown by single planes. But not every airplane in the skies over Afghanistan was dropping bombs or launching missiles. In fact, out of the total sorties flown only 4,425 were made by bombers and fighters. Flying in support of coalition combat operations were a variety of aircraft ranging from airborne tankers and cargo transports to radar-jamming planes and special-operations helicopters. The crews of these aircraft demonstrated the same accomplished flying skills and faced the same dangers of being in a war zone as did the combat pilots. And their missions were every bit as vital to the success of the war on terrorism.

Mercy Flights

Dim red lights, a color that will not interfere with the crew's night vision, illuminate the interior of the aircraft. It is unpressurized at an altitude of more than twenty-five thousand feet, and the crew must wear oxygen masks in the cold, thin air. In the night sky outside, the plane's running lights are extinguished to make it harder for antiaircraft crews on the ground to see it. Flying high over the Afghanistan countryside, this mission will keep the aircraft aloft for some sixteen hours. But the plane's crew is used to the long haul. "I've been flying for eighteen years," said one crewman, "and this is a tough task. But it's what we've been trained for." [33] Somewhere over northern Afghanistan the aircraft nears the target area and it is time for action. Soon the plane slows and the pilot pulls back on the control wheel, bringing the aircraft to a slight nose-up attitude. At a prearranged moment a signal light turns green and the payload falls away from the aircraft, heading for its target far below. As it makes a wide turn and heads for home another C-17 Globemaster III has just delivered 17,220 packages of food to the Afghans, a people devastated by poverty, oppression, and war.

From the beginning of the war on terrorism U.S. aircraft dropped not only bombs on Afghanistan but food and medicine as well. One of the primary vehicles for the humanitarian side of the operation was the C-17 Globemaster III. "From the very first bomb drop," says General John W. Handy, commander of the U.S. Transportation Command, "Air Force C-17s . . . were flying over the northwestern part of Afghanistan . . . in a combat environment with no assurance what it was going to be like."[34] Designed and built by the Boeing Aircraft Company as a versatile troop and cargo transport, the Globemaster made its first flight in 1991 and joined the U.S. Air Force arsenal in 1993. The C-17 is 174 feet long and has a wingspan of 170 feet, with a distinctive "T" tail that towers 55 feet above the ground. Powered by four turbofan engines, the Globemaster cruises around 28,000 feet at more than five hundred miles per hour. It is suitable for a variety of missions and can carry 102 troops, 90 wounded soldiers and their attendants, or up to 170,900 pounds of cargo. The C-17's flexibility, large cargo capacity, and low maintenance requirements made it ideal for Operation Enduring Freedom's humanitarian mission.

Inside the Globemaster's cargo hold, forty-two large cargo boxes are lined up and secured to the aircraft with canvas straps. The boxes, known as TRIAD, or tri-walled air delivery boxes, are about eighty inches high and four feet on a side—they look much like refrigerator delivery cartons. Inside each TRIAD box are 410 humanitarian daily rations (HDRs), each one containing a day's worth of food for one person. The HDRs include a vegetarian meal with rice, beans, a fruit bar, and other items. Along with the food, the HDRs contain a message printed on their bright yellow packages: "A Food Gift from the People of the United States of America." As the plane nears the drop site, usually near Afghan refugee camps, the large rear cargo door of the C-17 is opened and the TRIAD boxes roll out the back of the plane. Once they leave the aircraft the boxes break apart and the HDRs float harmlessly to the ground. On a calm night the packages can cover an area of about one by two miles; in windy conditions the drop zone may stretch as far as three miles.

Much controversy has surrounded the humanitarian food drop program. Some relief agencies have said that the airdrops are just propaganda, while others contended that ground shipments rather than airdrops are the only way to get enough food to the starving Afghan masses. Nevertheless, humanitarian aid continued throughout Operation Enduring Freedom. On October 31, 2001, the one millionth HDR was dropped from a C-17 Globemaster over Afghanistan. More than 2.4 million rations were ultimately delivered, along with wheat, blankets, and clothing, during 198 missions. "It was an extraordinary team effort," says one Globemaster commander. "All the missions were completed without injury or mishap."[35] And the C-17s did their part to assure the success of the humanitarian mission. Says General Handy, "We

Airdrops for Life

It may not seem like much of a meal for the average American, but the humanitarian daily rations dropped over Afghanistan can mean the difference between eating and starving to thousands of Afghan refugees. Humanitarian daily rations (HDRs) were developed after the Persian Gulf War of 1991, when U.S. officials began looking for ways to feed refugees in northern Iraq. They tried the standard military ration known as an MRE or Meal, Ready-to-Eat, but found that these meals sometimes contained pork, which for religious reasons cannot be eaten by Muslims. In 1993 the HDR was developed to provide a twenty-two-hundred-calorie meal, a full day's requirement, for one person. In accordance with sometimes strict religious and cultural restrictions, it contains no animal products, no alcohol, and a minimal amount of dairy products. The HDR may be eaten cold or heated over a fire or in hot water. Instructions for opening and eating the meal are printed in several languages and in pictures on the container. It can be stored for up to thirty-six months without spoiling. Each humanitarian daily ration costs about four dollars to produce.

A typical humanitarian daily ration will contain the following: barley stew, rice and vegetables in sauce, vegetable biscuits, jam, peanut butter, fruit bar, shortbread cookies, fruit pastry, and accessory pack containing salt, pepper, a spoon, matches, a moist towelette, and a napkin. Several different menus have been developed to provide variety for the refugees who will eat the meals.

The HDR program has come under some criticism by humanitarian groups who say that it does not contain the proper items for a Muslim population. Indeed, most Afghans who open the packages have never seen peanut butter and do not know what to do with it. Some who try it do not like it, although many have found that their donkeys enjoy the treat. Another problem with airdropping the HDRs is that malnourished refugees are less likely to be able to retrieve the packages; the able-bodied can beat them to the rations. And

many of the HDRs find their way not to local people but to the local market, where they are sold to those who can afford them.

Still, for the U.S. airmen and women who drop the packages, the hope remains that most of the HDRs will reach the people who need them the most. "I like the idea of what we're doing," one C-17 loadmaster told the *Charleston Post and Courier* (www.charleston.net). "It really brings it home when I see the video of kids picking up the food packets off the ground. It means we're making a difference."

A soldier collects packets of Humanitarian Daily Rations to give to Afghan villagers.

are just amazed at how well the aircraft has performed during OEF." [36]

Another support aircraft that saw duty in a variety of ways in the war on terrorism was the C-130 Hercules.

One Plane—Many Roles

No aircraft played more roles in the war on terrorism than the C-130 Hercules. In fact, it is probably the most versatile tactical aircraft ever built, with capabilities ranging from troop and cargo transport to electronic warfare, aerial helicopter refueling, search and rescue, special-operations missions, and even the recovery of space capsules. This is an impressive record of accomplishments for an airplane that first joined the air force in 1956 and is still going strong.

The Lockheed C-130 was originally designed as a medium transport aircraft for delivering troops and equipment into battle zones. Smaller than the newer C-17 Globemaster, the Hercules has a wingspan of 133 feet and a fuselage 98 feet long. As a tactical aircraft, the C-130 can take off and land on dirt strips as well as on paved runways. Like the Globemaster, it is a high-wing aircraft, meaning the wings are attached to the top of the fuselage. Powered by four turboprop engines turning 13.5 foot-diameter propellers, the "Herc" has a maximum cruising speed of around four hundred miles per hour and a cruising altitude of twenty-eight thousand feet. It can carry a normal payload of around twenty-eight thousand pounds of cargo—paratroopers or ground combat troops, medical stretch-

ers, armored vehicles, or even helicopters. The C-130 normally carries a crew of at least four: two pilots, a flight engineer, and a loadmaster who is in charge of the cargo. Specialized missions may call for additional personnel such as a navigator and extra loadmaster for airdrop sorties. One unique task performed by the C-130 during Operation Enduring Freedom was its use as a flying radio station.

Information from Aloft

The name sounds like it should belong to a comic book superhero: Commando Solo. But in reality it is the designation for a unique task assigned to the 193rd Special Operations Wing of the Pennsylvania Air National Guard. Commando Solo is a psychological operations (PSYOP) mission that broadcasts information by AM and FM radio and television in situations of national emergency anywhere in the world. The broadcasts originate from an E-C-130 aircraft (a specially modified C-130) flying over hostile countries. "It's amazing the effect that truthful, accurate information has on people," says Colonel Frank Goldstein, commander of the Air Intelligence Agency. "PSYOP has time and time again proven its worth, and the EC-130 is a key part of our overall strategy." [37] In the initial bombing of Afghanistan, Taliban-controlled radio stations broadcasting anti-U.S. propaganda were silenced. Soon Commando Solo broadcasts were filling the air.

Inside a Commando Solo E-C-130 (there are six in the 193rd Wing's fleet), the cargo area resembles a broadcast control room. Audio and video recorders are installed in racks along the sides of the aircraft, along with transmitters and other equipment used to beam and monitor the signal transmitted to the audience far below. Broadcast antennae are located in pods on the tail and under the wings of the E-C-130, while other wire antennae are unreeled below or behind the aircraft. Several radio and television signals can be transmitted at one time. In addition to the regular crew, five specialists operate the electronic communications systems.

During flights over Afghanistan, Commando Solo aircraft flew with fighter escorts for protection. Messages developed by the U.S. Army Fourth Psychological Operations Group were broadcast in the Afghans' native language as the E-C-130s orbited their target audience. The messages ranged from informing refugees of the locations of humanitarian aid and the availability of rewards for information on terrorists, to warning civilians to stay away from potentially dangerous areas. One broadcast announced, "We have no wish to hurt you, the innocent people of Afghanistan. Stay away from military installations, government buildings, terrorist camps, roads, factories or bridges." [38] Messages were also broadcast to the Taliban, urging them to lay down their arms and surrender.

Broadcasting to the Enemy

Psychological warfare operations play an important role in any war. Broadcasting, leaflets dropped from aircraft, and other methods of propaganda can be used to try to turn an oppressed people against their rulers, generate support for an invading force, or simply explain that the ordinary citizens of a country at war are not being targeted. During Operation Enduring Freedom, Commando Solo aircraft broadcast such messages to the people of Afghanistan. Here is a sample transcript of one message beamed to the Taliban, urging them to surrender and posted on the CNN website on October 17, 2001, in Jamie McIntyre's article "U.S. Propaganda to Taliban":

Attention, Taliban! You are condemned. Did you know that? The instant the terrorists you support took over our planes, you sentenced yourselves to death. The Armed Forces of the United States are here to seek justice for our dead. Highly trained soldiers are coming to shut down once and for all Osama bin Laden's ring of terrorism, and the Taliban that supports them and their actions.

Our forces are armed with state of the art military equipment. What are you using, obsolete and ineffective weaponry? Our helicopters will rain fire down upon your camps before you detect them on your radar. Our bombs are so accurate we can drop them right through your windows. Our infantry is trained for any climate and terrain on earth. United States soldiers fire with superior marksmanship and are armed with superior weapons.

You have only one choice.... Surrender now and we will give you a second chance. We will let you live. If you surrender no harm will come to you. When you decide to surrender, approach United States forces with your hands in the air. Sling your weapon across your back muzzle towards the ground. Remove your magazine and expel any rounds. Doing this is your only chance of survival.

A KC-135 Stratotanker refuels an F-16 Fighting Falcon.

One problem that Commando Solo mission planners had to confront was the fact that the Afghan people are so poor that few own radios. This was solved by air-dropping small radio receivers powered by a windup mechanism that eliminates the need for batteries or plug-in power. These simple radios are tuned to the frequency at which the Commando Solo signal is broadcast. Commando Solo flights continued until March 2002, when Afghan radio stations, no longer under Taliban control, resumed broadcasting.

Gas Stations in the Air

One reason for the success of Operation Enduring Freedom was the ability to refuel attack planes, bombers, and other aircraft in midflight. More than 13,600 aerial tanker flights were made during Operation Enduring Freedom—about three refueling flights for every combat sortie flown. The air force's primary refueling aircraft is the KC-135 Stratotanker.

Like much of today's air force arsenal the KC-135 is an experienced veteran, having joined the fleet in 1957. While its main job is as an aerial refueler, the KC-135 can also carry up to eighty-three thousand pounds of cargo or thirty-seven passengers on a cargo deck above the fuel tanks. The Stratotanker can carry up to two hundred thousand pounds of aviation fuel (the military often measures fuel in pounds rather than gallons) to deliver to various air force, navy, and marine aircraft. Fuel transfer takes place via a long boom that extends out the back of the KC-135. Small vanes attached to the boom allow an operator to control it as the aircraft to be refueled approaches. The operator lies on his stomach in the rear of the plane, looking out a window and "flying" the boom to make the connection with the aircraft being refueled. Midair refueling operations call for precision flying on the parts of both the Stratotanker pilot and the pilot of the plane receiving the fuel. The two aircraft must maintain a distance of only about fifty feet between them and hold it for the fifteen to twenty minutes it takes to complete the transfer. Nighttime operations add even more difficulty to the already challenging task. "You're low on gas, it's dark, the tankers have their lights on very low, if at all," recalls an F/A-18 pilot who had gone through numerous refuelings over Afghanistan. "It's not easy, especially when it gets turbulent. Sometimes it's more difficult than finding a target and dropping a bomb on it." [39]

Along with the venerable KC-135s, other tankers are helping to keep fighters and bombers in the sky over Afghanistan. The KC-10, an aerial tanker based on the civilian DC-10 airliner, is called the Extender for its ability to extend the flight range of military aircraft from all service branches. Larger that the KC-135, the KC-10 can carry a fuel load of 356,000 pounds in its seven fuel tanks. Like the Stratotanker, the Extender also has the ability to transport cargo and passengers in its cargo compartment above the fuel tanks. To extend its own range, the KC-10 can itself be refueled in flight by another KC-10 or a KC-135.

Aerial tankers, like any aircraft in a war zone, are in constant danger of being targeted by enemy radar on the ground or in hostile aircraft. One way to minimize that danger is to interfere with the enemy's radar signals. A navy plane nicknamed the Prowler is designed to do just that.

Electronic Warfare

Throughout the history of warfare, explosives and flying projectiles have been the major source of danger to soldiers and military vehicles. But the modern battlefield also has invisible hazards in the form of radar waves that can pinpoint aircraft and direct hostile fire toward a target with great accuracy. To combat this threat in Afghanistan the EA-6B Prowler took to the air to perform its unique mission: electronic countermeasures.

Although derived from the A-6 Intruder attack aircraft that flew in Vietnam and in the Persian Gulf War, the EA-6B carries few weapons. Instead, the Prowler is loaded with electronic equipment located in a pod at the tip of its tail fin and in additional pods attached under the wings and fuselage. These pods contain sensitive radar receivers to detect enemy radar signals, and transmitters to jam, or disrupt, the hostile emissions. Designed for carrier launch and operations from forward land bases, the twin-jet-engine EA-6B is manned by a crew of four: the pilot and three electronic-countermeasures officers (ECMOs). One ECMO sits next to the pilot and is responsible for the Prowler's navigation and communication. Behind these officers sit two more ECMOs who operate the plane's electronic warfare equipment, the centerpiece of which is the AN/ALQ-99 tactical jamming system. The AN/ALQ-99 is a computerized system that integrates the operation of the Prowler's various antennae, receivers, and transmitters to automatically detect hostile radar signals and transmit jamming signals to disrupt the radar beam. In addition to jamming radar, the Prowler can also disrupt enemy communications. According to a report by the Lexington Institute, a public policy research organization:

> In Operation Enduring Freedom, the Prowler exhibited the same tactical flexibility shown by other sea-based forces. Initially, it played a central role in suppressing enemy air defenses, enabling the other aircraft in coalition forces to safely penetrate Afghan airspace. Once air defenses were destroyed, it shifted

to jamming enemy communications on the ground, using both its dedicated communications-jamming suite and its improved radar-jamming equipment. [40]

But the Prowler can do more than just jam radar signals. When equipped with two AGM-88 HARM missiles it can also destroy the antennae transmitting the radar signals. The HARM, or high-speed antiradiation missile, is a fourteen-foot-long solid propellant air-to-surface missile carried under

An EA-6B Prowler takes off from Incirlik Air Base in Turkey.

the wings of the EA-6B and other aircraft. As a "defense suppression" weapon, the AGM-88's receivers pick up and lock onto an enemy radar signal and then home in on that signal to deliver the missile's 150-pound high-explosive payload. Even if the radar is shut down after the HARM has locked onto its signal, the missile's internal guidance system will direct it toward the target area with no great loss of precision.

The bombers, fighters, and support aircraft of Operation Enduring Freedom are known as fixed-wing aircraft. But rotary-wing aircraft, as helicopters are officially designated, also played an important part in the war on terrorism.

Versatile Birds

In the early weeks of Operation Enduring Freedom attack aircraft and bombers used their speed, high-altitude capability, and heavy bomb loads to deliver devastating

blows to the Taliban and al-Qaeda. As the enemy ground defenses dwindled, helicopters could begin to contribute their own unique advantages to the war effort. With their ability to fly low and slow, to take off and land vertically, and to navigate mountainous terrain, helicopters proved their mettle as versatile multirole weapons and support platforms in Afghanistan.

Black Hawks at War

On October 19, 2001, one hundred U.S. Army Rangers launched raids on targets near Kandahār, the first special forces troops to see action in the war in Afghanistan. These troops were transported into Afghanistan by UH-60 Black Hawk helicopters, the rotary-wing utility workhorse of the U.S. Army. First flown in 1974 and deployed by the army four years later, the Black Hawk uses two turboshaft engines to turn its fifty-four-foot main rotor. An eleven-foot tail ro-

Special-Ops Helicopters

Before the elite troops of special-operations forces can go to work behind enemy lines, they must get there, swiftly, silently, and undetected. One of the vehicles used to perform these important yet dangerous transport missions in Afghanistan was the U.S. Air Force MH-53 Pave Low helicopter.

The largest and most sophisticated helicopter in the air force arsenal, the Pave Low is a twin-engine rotary-wing aircraft that can deliver up to thirty-eight special-operations troops into a target area day or night in virtually any weather. It is armor-plated and carries three 7.62 mm miniguns, three .50 caliber machine guns, or a combination

of these weapons. Capable of refueling in midair, the MH-53 has a virtually unlimited range. First deployed in 1981, the Pave Low has seen action in the Persian Gulf War of 1991, as well as in Panama, Iraq, and Serbia. Besides infiltrating and exfiltrating special-operations troops, the MH-53 is used for the search and rescue of downed pilots, in humanitarian airlift operations, and as a recovery vehicle for the U.S. space program.

After the terrorist attacks of September 11, 2001, Pave Lows were on the scene within six hours, assisting in the rescue effort. In support of Operation Enduring Freedom, they flew more than one thousand combat hours over Afghanistan.

tor provides additional lift and counteracts the torque of the main rotor. Depending on its mission the Black Hawk is operated by a crew of three or four and can transport eleven soldiers in full field gear into battle zones. As an aircraft that must fly low and drop into "hot" landing zones where the enemy is active, the UH-60 is armor-plated to withstand hostile fire. The two pilot seats have additional armor plating, and the cockpit doors and canopy are made with Kevlar, the material used in bulletproof vests. Even the titanium and fiberglass rotor blades can take a hit from a 23 mm shell without sustaining damage. Active defense systems include electronic countermeasures and flare and chaff dispensers to confuse enemy radar.

In addition to its defensive armor and equipment, the Black Hawk also carries offensive armament. Doorway mounts can accommodate two .50 caliber or 7.62 mm machine guns, while up to sixteen AGM-114 Hellfire antiarmor missiles can be mounted on an external frame. The Black Hawk can also be equipped with several other types of missiles, mine dispensers, and external fuel tanks for varied missions.

The versatile UH-60 has found a place in other branches of the military besides the army, modified to suit the specific needs of the other services. The air force's version, the HH-60 Pave Hawk, is used for search and rescue of downed air crews, medical evacuation, civilian disaster relief, and support for NASA's space shuttle missions. The U.S. Navy uses its SH-60 Sea Hawk for anti-submarine and antiship warfare, cargo transport, and special forces operations.

Apaches and Cobras

For sheer firepower the AH-64 Apache and AH-1 Cobra are attack helicopters that bring a deadly punch to the battlefield. They saw action during Operation Anaconda, the assault on Taliban and al-Qaeda strongholds in the eastern Afghanistan mountains in March 2002. The Apache is the army's primary attack helicopter and can operate day or night in almost all types of weather. The twin-engine Apache is operated by a crew of two sitting in tandem, the pilot slightly higher in the rear of the cockpit, with the copilot/gunner in the front seat. The AH-64 is designed to absorb combat damage and remain airborne; it can continue to operate for thirty minutes after losing all its oil. Cruising at a speed of more than 170 miles per hour, the Apache can mount sixteen Hellfire antiarmor missiles or seventy-six smaller Hydra folding fin rockets for attacks against personnel and lightly armored vehicles. A target acquisition designation sight incorporates optical sensors and laser range finding and target designation for the Hellfire missiles. The pilot night-vision sensor links infrared sensors on the front of the Apache to a display in the pilots' helmets. Wherever the pilots turn their heads the sensors follow, allowing navigation and fire control at night or in adverse weather conditions.

In the opening hours of Operation Anaconda, U.S. and al-Qaeda troops were

An AH-64 Apache helicopter flies past a village on its way to Kandahār.

often in such close proximity that bombing the enemy by jets was out of the question. But the situation was ideal for the Apache. "The weapon that changed the face of the battle for us was the Apache,"[41] comments Colonel Frank Wiercinski, commander of the U.S. troops in the battle.

The AH-1W Super Cobra attack helicopter was flown by U.S. Marines during Operation Anaconda. Similar in appearance to the Apache, the all-weather, twin-engine helicopter is armed with a 20 mm three-barrel Gatling gun mounted under the nose, and a variety of missiles can be mounted externally for assaults on armored vehicles and bunkers. The AH-1W uses laser and infrared targeting systems for aiming its missiles and has chaff and flare dispensers for self-defense. In Operation Anaconda, Super Cobras provided air support for U.S. troops, firing on enemy mortar positions, attacking cave complexes, and flushing Taliban and al-Qaeda troops out of hiding.

Transporting the Troops

The job of getting troops to the mountainous battlefield area of Operation Anaconda, and getting them out again, fell to the huge U.S. Army CH-47 and MH-47 Chinook helicopters. The Chinook is a twin-engine heavy-lift cargo helicopter with two three-bladed rotors located on pylons at the front and rear of the aircraft. First delivered to the army in 1962 for the Vietnam War, the Chinook is operated by a two-man crew and can deliver from thirty-three to forty-four combat troops to a battle zone. Chinooks also brought ammunition and other vital cargo to the troops, relying on their high-altitude capabilities to operate in the mountains of eastern Afghanistan. An advanced multi-mode terrain-following and terrain-avoidance radar in the MH-47 (the special-operations version of the Chinook) allows it to fly at low levels in zero-visibility conditions caused by fog, sandstorms, or darkness.

Flying into battle zones can be just as dangerous for transport aircraft as it is for helicopter gunships, as Chinook crews soon found out in Operation Enduring Freedom. "When we fly around at 200, 300 feet," says Captain Kevin Cochie, a Chinook pilot, "you can hit us with a shotgun."[42] The reality of that danger became apparent when seven servicemen on two Chinooks were killed on March 4, 2002, during Operation Anaconda.

When the first Chinook was hit and disabled by a rocket-propelled grenade, a navy SEAL died after he fell out of the helicopter. The second Chinook, coming to the aid of the first, was hit by machine-gun fire and made a "hard landing." Fierce enemy fire kept the crew and the troops they were transporting pinned down. When rescue finally came twelve hours later, four soldiers and two air force men, in addition to the navy SEAL, had been killed, and eleven more were wounded.

Despite the danger faced by their pilots and crews, support aircraft and helicopters were just as vital to the success of Operation Enduring Freedom as were the more "glamorous" fighters and bombers. Another vital aspect of the war on terrorism dealt not with the thunder of rockets and bombs, but with the quiet and clandestine collecting of information.

Chapter 5

Gathering Intelligence

In order for a nation to pursue a large military campaign, vast amounts of information must be gathered, evaluated, and then disseminated to the proper personnel for integration into a plan of action. If a general or admiral can determine what his enemy's plans are, or how an enemy is positioned on the battlefield, he can assemble his own forces to counter the enemy threat. Gathering information has been an important aspect of warfare since antiquity. As Sun-tzu, an ancient Chinese general, wrote in the fourth century B.C., "A hundred ounces of silver spent for information may save ten thousand spent on war."[43]

One of the most effective ways of learning what the enemy is doing is to take to the air and evaluate the situation on the battlefield from a high vantage point. Ever since the Civil War, when the Union army sent photographers up in hot-air balloons to take pictures of the Confederate lines, aerial reconnaissance has been an integral part of military strategy. As the world entered the age of rockets and satellites, space became a new frontier for aerial reconnaissance. "From a military point of view, space is the ultimate high ground,"[44] says General Ralph E. Eberhart, commander of the North American Aerospace Defense Command.

During Operation Enduring Freedom the United States used many high-tech methods of collecting this information, which is known in the military as intelligence. Some of those methods involved observing the war in Afghanistan from hundreds of miles in space.

Eyes in Space

The United States had been thinking about building a spy satellite even before the first artificial satellite—the Soviet Union's *Sputnik*—was blasted into orbit in October 1957. Just weeks after *Sputnik*'s beeps from space proclaimed the Soviet triumph, the U.S. spy satellite program was given the go-ahead. Code named Corona, the project called for a series of satellites to be launched into orbit with an onboard camera to take photographs of Earth below. Using satellites to gather photographic information for military use is called "image intelligence." The Corona satellite's high-resolution camera, designated Keyhole, would shoot black-and-white pictures of our Cold War adversary, the Soviet Union, looking for missile launchers, airfields, and other potential military targets. After the film was exposed, its protective canister would then be ejected from the satellite to float toward Earth on parachutes. A specially designed cargo aircraft would snag the canister in midair and reel it into the cargo bay for delivery to the National Reconnaissance Office (NRO) for processing and evaluation. Established in 1960, the NRO's mission is to oversee all U.S. satellite and spy plane missions.

Corona's system of dropping and catching film canisters was cumbersome but it worked, proving the value of space-based intelligence gathering. Although the last Corona mission took place in 1972, Keyhole camera systems continued to fly into space throughout the 1980s and 1990s and into the twenty-first century. As technology advanced, the Keyhole cameras went from using ordinary film to employing sophisticated digital imaging systems that transmitted pictures to another satellite, which

The Spy Alphabet

Espionage is an integral part of warfare, and the war on terrorism is no exception. But just as there are many methods used to spy on an enemy (from satellites in space to telephone wiretaps), there are also numerous intelligence organizations that are charged with actually conducting spy missions. The following information is from *Spy Book: The Encyclopedia of Espionage,* by Norman Polmar and Thomas B. Allen.

CIA (Central Intelligence Agency): Successor to World War II's Office of Strategic Services, the CIA conducts worldwide collection and evaluation of intelligence, mainly through covert, or secret, activities.

DIA (Defense Intelligence Agency): The DIA was established in 1961 to coordinate the intelligence activities for the military services; it also provides intelligence for UN peacekeeping forces.

FBI (Federal Bureau of Investigation): Operating within the United States, the FBI is the principal U.S. counterespionage agency, investigating the violation of U.S. espionage laws by foreign spies.

NRO (National Reconnaissance Office): Under the Department of Defense, the NRO oversees the design, development, and operation of U.S. spy satellites.

NPIC (National Photographic Interpretation Center): This agency analyzes photographs taken from spy satellites and reconnaissance aircraft such as the U-2.

NSA (National Security Agency): This organization's primary mission is to gather signals intelligence (SIGINT), such as information gathered by intercepting radio communications and tapping telephones. The NSA's Central Security Service is the agency's code-breaking arm.

in turn relayed the images to a ground station for recording. These electronic images could be available for interpretation in a matter of hours rather than the days it took to develop and distribute film.

Picture resolution also improved. The first Keyhole camera, KH-1, could see objects on the ground that were no smaller than forty feet on a side. The latest version of the satellite, designated Advanced KH-11, can see objects on the ground as small as four to six inches across. The thirty-six-thousand-pound satellite measures about fifty feet long and fifteen feet in diameter and is launched into orbit from Vandenberg Air Force Base in California. It is similar to the Hubble Space Telescope, but points at Earth rather than into outer space. Two large mirrors gather and focus light onto the image sensor, a charge-coupled device similar to the imaging chips found in home video cameras. The KH-11 has both optical and infrared sensors that allow it to shoot pictures day or night, revealing Taliban troop movements, vehicles, al-Qaeda terrorist camps, and other important military information. The movement of vast numbers of Afghan refugees could also be monitored to help ground forces avoid attacking these noncombatants.

A satellite image reveals the location of a terrorist training camp in Afghanistan.

Spying with IKONOS

The exceptional capabilities of the Advanced KH-11 made it a valuable reconnaissance tool; three of the satellites were used to provide photographic intelligence in support of Operation Enduring Freedom. But not all spy satellites that took reconnaissance photographs of the evolving war in Afghanistan were military. In September 1999 the first commercial Earth-observing satellite was launched into orbit aboard an Athena II rocket. Named IKONOS (technically IKONOS II, since the first one, IKONOS I, malfunctioned and burned up reentering the earth's atmosphere), the satellite was built for Space Imaging Corporation in Colorado. IKONOS's highly polished mirrors reflect light into its electro-optical image sensors for processing and transmission to ground stations. The sixteen-hundred-pound satellite orbits Earth at a distance of 423 miles,

Smoke rises from the debris of the World Trade Center in this IKONOS image.

passing over every region on Earth an average of twice a day, capturing a visual path more than 6 miles wide. The IKONOS camera can produce black-and-white images at a resolution of one meter (3.3 feet) and color images at four meters (just over 13 feet).

Images from IKONOS are available for sale to the public and are useful in a wide range of disciplines: urban planning, crop forecasting, monitoring the environment, and oil exploration, among others. But one day after the terrorist attacks of September 11, 2001, IKONOS flew over New York and captured some new and disturbing images: the smoking ruins of the site where the World Trade Center towers had once stood. Space Imaging Corporation made its photographs of the World Trade Center, both before and after the attacks, available for free on the Internet.

When Operation Enduring Freedom began, IKONOS, a civilian satellite, was drafted into military service. Starting on October 7, 2001, the U.S. military purchased exclusive rights to the images that IKONOS took of Afghanistan to help in the war on terrorism. "They are buying all the imagery that is available," said John Copple, the head of Space Imaging Corporation. "And they're using it for maps, they're using it for planning, they're using it for damage assessment after they run missions—they're using it in a variety of ways."[45] While the resolution of the IKONOS images is not as good as that of the KH-11 satellites (three feet versus six inches), they provided additional "eyes" on the battlefields of Operation Enduring Freedom. And there was another advantage to the exclusive military use of IKONOS images—they were prevented from falling into enemy hands. "We don't want the media to run satellite photos that can be interpreted by terrorists and place our forces in harm's way,"[46] explained a Department of Defense spokesman.

The military contract with Space Imaging lasted three months, after which some IKONOS photographs of Afghanistan began appearing on the Internet. Images of Taliban missile launching sites, armored vehicles, airfields, and terrorist training camps were shown both before and after strikes by U.S. and coalition forces. The photographs show the pinpoint accuracy achieved by smart munitions as they took out their targets with minimal damage to surrounding areas.

While spy satellites were focusing their cameras on the battlefields far below, other satellites were providing information that let troops know where they, and their targets, were located.

Navigating from Space

In the first week of Operation Enduring Freedom aircraft dropped about five hundred joint direct-attack munitions (JDAMs, or smart bombs) on military targets in Afghanistan. The bombs knew exactly where their targets were thanks to twenty-four satellites orbiting some 12,500 miles above Earth. These satellites, called Navstar, make up the worldwide network of navigation coordinates known as the Global Positioning System (GPS). Developed by the military to provide improved land coordinates and targeting information for its combat operations, the Global Positioning System is now available to civilians as well. GPS receivers can be found in airplanes, ships, trucks, and personal automobiles, and handheld models are popular among hikers and other sportsmen. Indeed, some experts believe small GPS units were used by the terrorists in their attacks on the World Trade Center and the Pentagon.

The twenty-four Navstar GPS satellites orbit Earth once every twelve hours following six different orbital paths, with four satellites following each path. As they circle the globe they transmit a continuous stream of coded radio signals that can be picked up by ground receivers. The orbits are calculated so that signals from five to eight GPS satellites are available at all times at any point on the globe. As they fly overhead, the Navstar satellites constantly calculate their positions in space and the time it takes for their signals to reach Earth. A GPS receiver must obtain signals from at least three satellites to establish the location of any position on Earth (or above Earth in the case of aircraft GPS receivers). The exact time and the

Navstar GPS personnel display ground-based receivers that pick up signals from satellites.

velocity of the receiver, if it is moving, can also be calculated. Accuracy of the Global Positioning System is astonishingly precise. Civilian users can obtain GPS information to locate their positions within approximately 130 feet. Military users have access to even more precise positioning information, allowing their locations to be calculated with an accuracy of about 20 feet.

It is this accuracy as well as the around-the-clock availability of information that makes GPS valuable in the war on terrorism. According to General Ralph E. Eberhart, "GPS is absolutely critical to U.S. military operations."[47] Smart bombs dropped on Afghanistan during the air campaign of Operation Enduring Freedom, including the JDAMs guided by the Global Positioning System, resulted in a greater number of direct hits on military targets. In addition to its use in air operations, GPS was employed in the ground war to allow troops to determine their own locations as well as the positions of enemy forces.

More Eyes in Space

Along with IKONOS and Navstar, other types of satellites played a part in Operation Enduring Freedom. One of the problems that satellites such as IKONOS and KH-11 encounter in taking photographs from space is poor weather. Radar-imaging satellites such as the *Lacrosse* can see objects as small as three feet across on the ground regardless of the weather or time of day. The satellite can detect military vehicles even if they are hidden by trees, and can reveal enemy troop movements at night. Satellites of the Defense Meteorological Satellite Program, as well as civilian weather satellites, tracked the weather over Afghanistan to assist in the planning of air strikes. Signal intelligence (SIGINT) satellites can eavesdrop on various wireless communication devices from military satellite communications to ordinary cell phones. After the terrorist attacks of September 11 several of America's SIGINT satellite orbits were adjusted to take them over Afghanistan in an effort to find Osama bin Laden.

During Operation Enduring Freedom satellites provided information from space, the "new high ground." But not all information came from such a lofty vantage point. Aircraft still contributed much useful intelligence for the military. Not long after Operation Enduring Freedom began, several strange-looking aircraft were seen flying through the skies over Afghanistan.

Planes Without Pilots

The idea of a pilotless military aircraft has been around since the early twentieth century. In 1917 the U.S. Navy experimented with an unmanned seaplane. Fourteen years later Great Britain flew its first reusable unmanned aircraft; the United States followed suit in 1935. A few pilotless planes flew during World War II and, as the technology advanced, more were used during the Vietnam and Persian Gulf Wars. Known as unmanned aerial vehicles, or UAVs, these small, rugged aircraft saw action in Operation Enduring Freedom.

The RQ-1A Predator UAV looks less like a military aircraft than an oversized model airplane. But with its forty-eight-foot wingspan and length of twenty-seven feet it will not be mistaken for a toy. The Predator stands more than six feet tall on the ground, supported by spindly landing gear. In the rear of the aircraft two tail fins droop down in an inverted V configuration, and a propeller at the tail "pushes" the plane through the air. The RQ-1A is powered by a one hundred horsepower Rotax engine similar to the engine found in a snowmobile. It cruises at a speed of about eighty-five miles per hour and operates at altitudes of up to twenty-five thousand feet. Smaller and lighter than a manned airplane, the Predator aircraft costs $3 million to $5 million, depending on how it is equipped. But it is part of a $25 million system that includes four aircraft, a ground control station, and a satellite link.

The Predator's flat-bottomed fuselage bulges at the front to accommodate the plane's satellite dish antenna. Also on board are 450 pounds of electronic and optical sensors, including a color TV camera in the nose for navigation, a daylight TV camera, an infrared imaging camera for nighttime or low-light surveillance, and a synthetic-aperture radar for imaging in cloudy or hazy conditions. To operate the Predator, the pilot sits in the ground control station and "flies" the aircraft just as if he were sitting in it, remotely maneuvering the aircraft with a joystick as he watches a color television image from the Predator's nose cam-

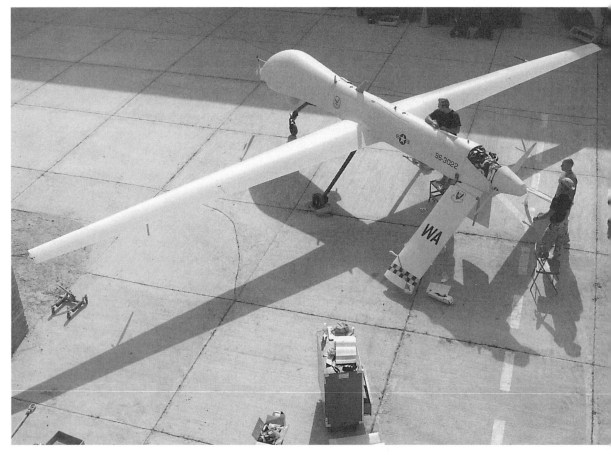

Crew members perform pre-flight checks on an RQ-IA Predator UAV prior to a mission.

era. Some pilots find it more difficult to fly than a conventional aircraft because the sensations of flying are not there. "You are aware that what you're controlling is a real aircraft," says air force lieutenant colonel Eric Mathewson. "It's more challenging than landing an F-15. There's no sound, no 'seat-of-the-pants' feel to it, and the peripheral vision is limited."[48] Being remotely controlled, the Predator is also safer: If shot down, the loss is only a $5 million plane, not a $30 million fighter and, possibly, a pilot's life.

As many as twelve Predators performed missions for Operation Enduring Freedom, operated by both the air force and the Central Intelligence Agency, America's spy agency. These included surveillance of enemy troop and convoy movements, monitoring the border between Afghanistan and Pakistan to search for escaping al-Qaeda terrorists, and providing targeting information for AC-130 gunships and other

Miniature Spies in the Sky

As with most advances in engineering, the size of a particular technology usually decreases as its capabilities increase. The technology of aerial surveillance has undergone similar miniaturization. At twenty-seven feet long the Predator unmanned aerial vehicle (UAV) is tiny compared to the U-2 spy plane developed in the 1960s. But even the Predator may soon be considered a giant when compared to the latest trend in aerial reconnaissance: the micro UAV.

The micro UAV (sometimes called a micro air vehicle, or MAV) is under development by several industrial companies and universities. MAVs come in a variety of shapes: Some look like toy airplanes while others resemble small flying saucers. An MAV generally measures less than six inches in both length and wingspan, but within that small airframe resides a wealth of state-of-the-art miniaturized electronic components. An MAV carries electronics for flight control and navigation, an autopilot system, plus a miniature television camera that can re-

MAVs such as the Microbat (pictured) provide aerial surveillance.

lay color pictures of military targets. An electric motor powered by rechargeable batteries can keep the tiny aircraft aloft for up to thirty minutes.

What can such a tiny vehicle do? Aerial reconnaissance is its primary mission, but many other jobs are envisioned by engineers who are working to increase the MAV's capabilities. The following futuristic scenario is taken from "Micro Air Vehicles—Toward a New Dimension in Flight," a report by James M. McMichael and Michael S. Francis of the Defense Advanced Research Projects Agency:

> The small speck in the sky approaches in virtual silence, unnoticed by the large gathering of soldiers below. In flight, its tiny size and considerable agility evade all but happenstance recognition. After hovering for a few short seconds, it perches on a fifth floor window sill, observing the flow of men and machines on the streets below. Several kilometers away, the platoon leader watches the action on his wrist monitor. He sees his target and sends the signal. The tiny craft swoops down on the vehicle, alighting momentarily on the roof. It senses the trace of a suspected chemical agent and deploys a small tagging device, attaching it to the vehicle. Just seconds later it is back in the sky, vanishing down a narrow alley. Mission accomplished.

MAVs may also be fitted with sensors to detect the spread of toxic chemical or biological clouds, or even carry pheromone sensors to identify and follow a specific individual. If the visionary designers of MAVs are right, you will be able to hold the latest advances in aerial reconnaissance in the palm of your hand.

attack aircraft. According to a newspaper report, "On one occasion in Afghanistan a Predator supplied real-time video pictures of a nighttime Taliban convoy stopping at a hotel, enabling nearby F-15s to attack the building."[49] The Predator's ability to stay aloft for twenty-four hours and circle a location is one of its most valuable features. According to a Department of Defense official, the Predator can "park over the bad guys, watch them continually, never give them a break from [our monitoring] their activities and severely limit their ability to mount an effective threat."[50] But the Predator can do more than just watch the bad guys. In addition to its reconnaissance role, the RQ-1A can be fitted with two Hellfire missiles, one under each wing. A laser-guided, solid-propellant air-to-ground missile with a high-explosive warhead, the Hellfire was developed as an antiarmor missile to be fired from helicopters. These "weaponized" Predators are sometimes referred to as unmanned aerial combat vehicles.

In October 2001, Predators armed with Hellfires went into combat for the first time over Afghanistan, described by *Washington Post* reporter Thomas Ricks as a "revolutionary step in the conduct of warfare."[51] Their targets included al-Qaeda terrorist camps, military facilities, storage areas, and troops fleeing attacks. The next month, a Predator took part in an aerial raid on a house. According to a *New York Times* account, in this attack the Predator "relayed live video pictures of the scene to CIA and military officials, who called in strikes from a Navy F/A-18 fighter bomber. As people fled the building, the Predator opened fire on them with Hellfire missiles. Finally it circled over the area, assessing the damage."[52] Killed in the raid was al-Qaeda's military commander, Mohammed Atef. One year later, in November 2002, a Predator destroyed a military vehicle in Yemen carrying an associate of Osama bin Laden. It was the first use of a weaponized UAV outside of the Afghan theater of operations.

Global Hawk

The latest entry into the ranks of unmanned aerial vehicles is the RQ-4A Global Hawk, a "big brother" to the Predator. The Global Hawk's wingspan of 116 feet is longer than that of a Boeing 737 airliner and is made of a lightweight composite material for strength. Powered by a jet engine, the RQ-4A flies at nearly four hundred miles per hour and can operate at altitudes of up to sixty-five thousand feet—almost three times the ceiling of the Predator. One distinct advantage of the Global Hawk is its extended-range capability; in June 2001 an RQ-4A set a world record for UAVs by making a nonstop twenty-three-hour test flight from California to Australia. With its ability to stay aloft for up to thirty-eight hours, the Global Hawk may one day replace such high-altitude spy planes as the Cold War–era U-2. "With one aircraft," says Major Paul Daly, a Global Hawk operator, "I do the job of possibly three [conventional] aircraft by keeping it airborne longer."[53]

Like the Predator, the Global Hawk has a bulbous nose that houses a satellite dish. The plane's surveillance equipment includes a synthetic-aperture radar and high-resolution electro-optical and infrared sensors for all-weather reconnaissance. This high-tech gear can spot a small object from near the edge of space. "It's a revolution in the way we look at collecting reconnaissance and conducting air operations," commented

Lieutenant Colonel Doug Boone. "We can differentiate objects the size of a foot in length up to a hundred miles away."[54] In a twenty-four-hour period the Global Hawk can survey an area on the ground totaling more than fifty thousand square miles—about the size of the state of Illinois. Unlike its little brother, however, the Global Hawk is not flown by a pilot sitting in a ground control station. Instead, it relies on a predetermined mission plan programmed into its two onboard computers before takeoff. "When you start it up," says air force colonel Mike Guidry, a Global Hawk pilot, "the airplane runs a check of all its systems, just the way a pilot would do. You download the mission plan via computer. You say, 'We want you to image Kandahār and Tora Bora.'"[55] Two Global Hawks were originally deployed during Operation Enduring Freedom, but one crashed due to bad weather or mechanical problems in December 2001.

Guidance for takeoff and landing is provided by a ground station, which programs data from the Global Positioning System into the Global Hawk's four onboard GPS navigational systems. In another ground station, the mission control trailer, pilots monitor the progress of the mission and point the Global Hawk's sensors to gather the highest quality images. The images are then transmitted via satellite to field commanders who use this real-time information to plan their battle operations. During a mission, operators can alter the course and altitude of the RQ-4A, or even upload a new mission plan, by sending signals from the ground to the aircraft. Still, as Guidry remarks, "Global Hawk works best when you just sit back and let it fly itself."[56] Not only does the Global Hawk fly itself, it can also land itself in an emergency, using its GPS systems to touch down on any runway in the world.

With the successes of the Predator and Global Hawk in Afghanistan, many people see the pilotless aircraft as the future of military reconnaissance aviation. But there are still plenty of manned aircraft performing essential intelligence-gathering duties.

Rivets, Stars, and AWACS

While the KC-135 Stratotanker was refueling combat aircraft over Afghanistan, three of its sister ships were collecting information to help those combat planes find their targets. Like the Stratotanker, the RC-135 Rivet Joint, E-8C JSTARS, and E-3 Sentry aircraft are all based on the commercial Boeing 707 airframe. But each one played a unique part in intelligence gathering in Operation Enduring Freedom.

The RC-135 Rivet Joint reconnaissance plane is a signals intelligence (SIGINT) aircraft. Its job is to detect and identify various electronic and communication signals that make up the "electronic battlefield." The Rivet Joint carries a crew of up to thirty-two, including the flight crew and various electronic-warfare officers, intelligence personnel, and maintenance technicians, depending on the mission. Inside the aircraft a vast array of multiband receivers, antennae, and satellite data link equipment

Homeland Surveillance

The gathering of intelligence by the use of aircraft or unmanned aerial vehicles (UAVs) is not limited to wartime, nor is it the exclusive province of the military deployed overseas. Interest in new tools for domestic surveillance has become big business, especially after the September 11, 2001, terrorist attacks. And the same technology used by the military in the war on terrorism is starting to be employed by law enforcement officials and other government agencies in the search for terrorists at home.

According to "Airborne Law Enforcement," an article on the *Aviation Today* website, (www.aviationtoday.com), "The line between law enforcement and counterterrorism is becoming increasingly blurred." Law enforcement agencies use aircraft, primarily helicopters, to conduct antiterrorist patrols along power lines, nuclear power plants, bridges, and other potential terrorist targets. The helicopters used by police departments may be equipped with gyrostabilized binoculars, high-intensity spotlights, and forward-looking infrared, the same device used by military aircraft in Afghanistan for target acquisition.

The U.S. Border Patrol, the agency whose job is to protect our borders, is also occasionally using high-tech equipment to perform its mission. For example, UAVs help the agency survey the thousands of miles of Canadian and Mexican borders that they must currently patrol using helicopters and ground vehicles. In August 2002 the Border Patrol seized a cache of marijuana and several smugglers at the Canadian border with the help of Pioneer UAVs operated by U.S. Marines. The U.S. Coast Guard has plans for the future deployment of Global Hawk UAVs for maritime surveillance. With a limited number of helicopters and pilots to fly them, the coast guard hopes to see the UAVs fill the gaps in its mission to search for drug smugglers and provide search-and-rescue services. Other government agencies such as the Department of Transportation and the Department of Energy have also explored the roles that unmanned aerial vehicles might play in their agencies.

search the battlefield for radio, radar, satellite, or even cell phone transmissions and relay the information to military commanders who can then pinpoint the target and take action.

One aircraft that can receive information from the Rivet Joint is the E-3 Sentry airborne warning and control system aircraft (AWACS). Immediately identifiable by the large "flying saucer"–shaped rotating radar antenna on top of its fuselage, the AWACS's mission is to manage and control war in the air. It can track and identify enemy ships and planes within the range of its radar antenna, and forward this information to command posts on the ground. Among other duties during Operation Enduring Freedom, AWACS aircraft controlled fighter aircraft flying in support of C-17 transport planes dropping humanitarian daily rations to Afghan refugees.

The E-8C joint surveillance/target attack radar system (JSTARS) aircraft are long-range air-to-ground radar surveillance and battle management planes. As its name implies, the JSTARS is actually a joint army–air force system, with the E-8C as the airborne platform and an army ground station module for information receiving and processing. The JSTARS has a jam-resistant multimode radar system on board, which

An E-3 Sentry AWACS conducts a surveillance mission over Afghanistan.

is designed to detect both stationary and moving targets on the ground within a range of more than 150 miles. The radar is so sophisticated that it can differentiate between a truck and a tracked vehicle such as a tank. "JSTARS brings a capability to track vehicles in all weather," says Rear Admiral John Stufflebeem of the Joint Chiefs of Staff. "That will be helpful when you're looking for trucks or SUVs or others that are moving around."[57] The Taliban used pickup trucks and SUVs, often mounted with guns, as one means of transportation around Afghanistan.

With all the sophisticated means of gathering intelligence available to U.S. forces during Operation Enduring Freedom, perhaps the people who needed accurate information the most were those who went "in harm's way": the troops on the ground in Afghanistan.

Chapter 6

Special-Operations Forces

After undergoing twelve days of pounding by U.S. bombs and missiles, Taliban air defenses had been neutralized and strikes on the important cities of Kandahār, Mazār-e Sharīf, and the capital city of Kabul were continuing. Many al-Qaeda terrorist training camps had been bombed, and roads, airfields, military equipment, and communication facilities were also targets of American munitions. But despite the success of the air strikes, it was clear that the war would not be won by airpower alone. Although it meant U.S. casualties were likely to rise, ground troops would have to go into Afghanistan to fight alongside the ragtag opponents of the Taliban and track down the elusive al-Qaeda soldiers wherever they had taken refuge. However, a massive invading army would be ill suited for conquering an elusive enemy in the rugged Afghan terrain. In this case the most effective ground weapon would be highly trained human beings—the elite force of warriors who make up the special-operations forces.

A Proud History

The modern concept of a force of special troops waging unconventional warfare can be traced back to the French and Indian War in the 1750s. In that conflict, a volunteer company of colonial soldiers called Rogers' Rangers fought using tactics their commander, Major Robert Rogers, learned from Native Americans. These included keeping their movements secret, fighting from protective cover, and striking an enemy swiftly and without warning. Unconventional warfare continued in the American Revolution under Francis Marion, nicknamed the "Swamp Fox" by the British, and in the Civil War by Confederate colonel John Singleton Moseby. World War II saw an increased use of special-operations forces worldwide with such units as Merrill's Marauders, Darby's Rangers, and the Devil's Brigade.

The term "special forces" was officially used by the army for the first time in 1952 with the formation of a new unit designed

A navy SEAL provides cover as his unit advances on al-Qaeda and Taliban forces.

to wage unconventional war behind enemy lines. In the early 1960s President John F. Kennedy began expanding the special-operations forces that by then had been established by the army, navy, and air force. From Vietnam to Operation Allied Force in Kosovo special-operations soldiers have played an important but largely unseen role in America's conflicts. Operation Enduring Freedom proved to be no exception.

Rangers Lead the Way

On October 19, 2001, the first U.S. combat troops were deployed in Afghanistan. At a news conference the next day, Gen-

eral Richard Myers, chairman of the Joint Chiefs of Staff, announced the start of the ground war. "Yesterday U.S. military forces conducted ground operations in addition to our air operations in support of Operation Enduring Freedom. . . . U.S. forces were able to deploy, maneuver, and operate inside Afghanistan without significant interference from Taliban forces."[58] Among the U.S. forces deployed were more than one hundred members of the U.S. Army Rangers.

The Rangers are the army's fast-strike light infantry units, often called upon to be the first troops sent into a dangerous situation, as in Operation Enduring Freedom. While not strictly a special forces unit, the Rangers are nonetheless highly trained fighters under the auspices of the U.S. Special Operations Command along with the special forces of the army and other service branches. Their task is succinctly described by Lieutenant General Doug Brown, commander of the army's special operations: "When we call for the Army Rangers, we expect them to break things and hurt people."[59]

The seventy-fifth Ranger Regiment, headquartered at Fort Benning, Georgia, is made up of three battalions that can deploy anywhere in the world upon eighteen hours' notice. The mission of the Rangers is multifaceted. They must be able to quickly and quietly enter a hostile environment by land, sea, or air; secure their objective; and leave the scene just as quickly. They must conduct swift raids as well as larger-scale attack operations. They must also be able to recover equipment or personnel to avoid having them fall into the hands of the enemy.

Soldiers who aspire to wear the distinctive "Rangers" tab on their sleeve must go through a rigorous training course at Ranger School at Fort Benning. To be eligible for Ranger training a soldier must be in top physical condition and have learned the basics of parachuting—a necessary skill since Rangers are often air-dropped into enemy territory. During the three-phase training course, Ranger candidates are put through arduous physical challenges, including a

A team of U.S. Army Rangers patrols a swamp. Rangers are often the first unit sent into a dangerous situation.

sixteen-mile march, hand-to-hand combat training, obstacle course runs, and land navigation training. They learn how to conduct day and night reconnaissance and ambush patrols, handle small boats and operate in jungle or swamp environments, and master mountaineering techniques in full combat gear. The candidates are pushed to the limits of physical and mental endurance, conducting patrols with little sleep and minimal rations of food and water. "We stress them in all kinds of ways," says Ranger sergeant major Michael Kelso, who added that a Ranger "will continue his mission even if he has to crawl to the target." [60] The rugged training takes its toll on would-be Rangers: Two-thirds of the candidates do not make it through the course. For those who do, dangerous missions await them in faraway places such as Afghanistan.

Night Drop into Afghanistan

At about 11:00 P.M. on the night of October 19, 2001, more than one hundred U.S. Army Rangers parachuted into Afghanistan. Their objectives were a command-and-control compound near the Taliban stronghold of Kandahār and a small airfield in southern Afghanistan. After encountering limited Taliban resistance and inflicting casualties on the enemy in a small-arms firefight, Rangers secured their objectives. While the command compound was sometimes occupied by Taliban leader Mullah Mohammed Omar, General Myers commented that commanders "did not expect to find significant Taliban leadership at these positions." [61] The Rangers did find a cache of weapons that included ammunition, a machine gun, and rocket-propelled grenades, all of which they destroyed. Other items were seized and brought back for determination of their intelligence value. "We gathered some intelligence, which we're evaluating," said Myers. He also commented that this first raid "shows what we are capable of, at a time of our choosing, conducting the type of operations we want to conduct." [62]

The operation was not without U.S. casualties, however, as two soldiers were injured in the parachute drop. On the same night, a Black Hawk helicopter crashed, killing two Rangers. The search-and-rescue helicopter was standing by to assist in the operation if needed, and crashed across the Afghan border in Pakistan. Although the Taliban boasted that they shot down the helicopter, U.S. officials discounted their claim as being "absolutely false," calling the crash an unfortunate mishap.

The raid on October 19 involved a force of more than one hundred U.S. Army Rangers. For another special-operations group, a typical operation consists of a team of only twelve highly trained soldiers. Their expertise is rigorously earned but usually hidden; the most visible symbol the members of this group proudly display is their distinctive headgear.

The Green Berets

They call themselves the "quiet professionals." When called upon to do combat

Delta Force

The least known of all the special forces organizations is the army's ultrasecret counter-terrorist unit, First Special Forces Operational Detachment–Delta. So covert is this organization that the army does not even admit that it exists. More often referred to as Delta Force, this elite group of special-ops warriors was established during the 1970s as a response to worldwide terrorism. Airplane hijackings, assassinations, and other acts of terror were on the rise, sometimes even being played out on television. In 1972 eleven Israeli athletes were slain by Arab terrorists at the Olympic Games in Munich, Germany, an atrocity that shocked the world. A short time later the army realized the importance of combating terrorism, and eventually called on Green Beret colonel Charles Beckwith to form a unit of highly trained antiterrorist soldiers. Beckwith, a vet-

eran of the Vietnam War, had spent a year as an exchange officer with the British special-operations unit, the Special Air Service (SAS). After getting the green light from the army, in late 1977 Beckwith secretly established Delta Force with Fort Bragg, North Carolina, as its headquarters.

Soldiers hoping to become a part of Delta Force go through a rigorous training course held twice a year at Fort Bragg. Colonel Beckwith modeled the training course on the one used by the SAS. This reportedly includes weapons and parachute training, climbing and rappelling exercises for storming tall buildings, and close-quarters combat and hostage rescue missions played out in a training complex featuring simulations of a house, office, and a commercial airliner cabin. Trainees learn how to extricate hostages in various hazardous situations.

they are among the world's most skillful warriors. But they possess other skills that may seem to have nothing to do with warfare but in reality are vital to winning a war in a far-off land where the people are different and the customs unfamiliar to most Americans. They are the army's premier special forces organization, known the world over as the Green Berets.

The Green Berets traces its history to Colonel Aaron Bank, a World War II officer in the Office of Strategic Services (OSS), the wartime military intelligence agency. After the war, Bank had the idea of developing small teams of highly trained soldiers who would perform guerrilla operations behind enemy lines. He called his organization "special forces" and chose Fort Bragg in North Carolina as its headquarters. The first

special forces unit, the Tenth Special Forces Group (Airborne), was activated in June 1952 with a complement of ten soldiers. The next year special forces soldiers adopted the green beret as their unofficial headgear, but it was not until 1961 that the distinctive symbol became official. Since their inception the Green Berets have seen action all over the world, in conflicts from the Vietnam War to Operation Enduring Freedom. And while many aspire to wear the green beret, only a few of the toughest and smartest soldiers will make the grade.

Earning the Beret

The road to becoming a special forces soldier is an arduous and expensive proposition. "At a minimum," writes author Tom Clancy, "a successful training evolution for

The Special Forces Creed

It takes a person of special character to qualify to wear the Green Beret. Those character traits are set forth in the Special Forces Creed, below, from Fred J. Pushies's book, *U.S. Army Special Forces.*

> I am an American Special Forces soldier. A professional! I will do all that my nation requires of me.
>
> I am a volunteer, knowing well the hazards of my profession.
>
> I serve with the memory of those who have gone before me: Rogers' Rangers, Francis Marion, Moseby's Rangers, the First Special Service Forces and Ranger Battalions of World War II, the Airborne Ranger Companies of Korea. I pledge to uphold the honor and integrity of all I am—in all I do.
>
> I am a professional soldier. I will teach and fight wherever my nation requires. I will strive always to excel in every art and artifice of war.

> I know that I will be called upon to perform tasks in isolation, far from familiar faces and voices, with the help and guidance of my God.
>
> I will keep my mind and body clean, alert, and strong, for this is my debt to those with whom I serve. I will not bring shame upon myself or the forces.
>
> I will maintain myself, my arms, and my equipment in an immaculate state as befits a Special Forces soldier.
>
> I will never surrender though I be the last. If I am taken, I pray that I may have the strength to spit upon my enemy.
>
> My goal is to succeed in any mission—and live to succeed again.
>
> I am a member of my nation's chosen soldiery. God grant that I may not be found wanting, that I will not fail this sacred trust.

a single SF [special forces] soldier takes a full year, and costs a minimum of $100,000." [63] Training begins with a three-week entry-level course called Special Forces Assessment and Selection (SFAS), where applicants tackle obstacle courses and marches, navigation exercises, and stress events designed to test the men to their limits. Those who pass the SFAS (and only about half do) go on to a grueling "Q," or qualification, course. During this difficult three-phase course the prospective Green Beret will learn not only the leadership and combat skills necessary for a special forces soldier, but will also gain expertise in such specialized areas as communications, medical

operations, engineering, or weapons. The Q course ends with a final exam called Robin Sage, a nineteen-day simulated combat exercise that tests all of the candidates' skills and stamina. Played out in a ten-county area near Fort Bragg that is called "Pineland" for the exercise, Robin Sage enlists local civilian volunteers and law enforcement officers to take part in the exercise. The citizens of the fictitious country of Pineland assist the soldiers in "liberating" their imaginary homeland. As if to confirm the realistic nature of Green Beret training, the special forces mission in Afghanistan during Operation Enduring Freedom closely resembled the Robin Sage scenario.

Upon completing the Q course and successfully passing Robin Sage, candidates are awarded their coveted green berets. But their training is still not over. Every Green Beret must learn at least one foreign language and attends language school after completion of the Q course. They must also successfully complete an advanced parachute course; survival training at the Survival, Evasion, Resistance, and Escape School; and an underwater skills course teaching the use of self-contained underwater breathing apparatus, or SCUBA. Even after all this training is over, a Green Beret can spend up to six months a year refining the skills he has learned. A typical Green Beret is older than the average soldier, usually somewhere in his mid thirties, and is at least a sergeant in rank. He (women are not eligible for special forces duty) is highly intelligent although not necessarily a college graduate. Despite the popular portrayal of the Green Beret as a "super soldier," most are not physically imposing. "Some of these guys are 145

Green Berets salute the crowd at a parade. The Green Berets comprise the army's toughest and smartest soldiers.

pounds soaking wet," recalls a former Green Beret. "It's about brains."[64] Said another Green Beret serving in Afghanistan, "Our mission is not necessarily to outfight the enemy, although we can do that if we have to. We would rather outthink them."[65]

The grueling special forces training has but one purpose: to make the Green Beret ready for any assignment that he is called upon to do. On October 7, 2001, the first day of air raids on Afghanistan, General Richard Myers told reporters, "I want to remind you that while today's operations are visible, many other operations may not be so visible."[66] Such invisible operations by the Green Berets would ultimately bring down the Taliban regime.

A Special-Operations War

The extensive use of special forces in Afghanistan marked a new way of waging ground combat for the United States in the twenty-first century. In the Persian Gulf War of 1991, some five hundred thousand soldiers battled the forces of Iraq's dictator, Saddam Hussein. In Afghanistan, however, for the first time small teams of special-operations troops, rather than regular soldiers, constituted the main attack force on the ground. These teams, officially known as Operational Detachment Alpha (ODA) but popularly called "A-Teams," are made up of twelve Green Berets including a captain as team leader. Each man in the team has a different specialty, such as weapons, communication, medicine, intelligence, and engineering.

In Operation Enduring Freedom, A-Teams were inserted into Afghanistan by helicopter from bases in neighboring countries such as Pakistan, Uzbekistan, and Tajikistan, or from specialized aircraft carriers such as the USS *Kitty Hawk* in the Gulf of Arabia. The first team to enter Afghanistan, ODA 555, was secretly infiltrated by helicopter on October 19, 2001. Team 555 was the first of just over three hundred special forces soldiers who would help topple the Taliban. Once inside Afghanistan, ODA 555 began seeking out members of the local anti-Taliban fighters, the Northern Alliance.

The Northern Alliance is a group of rebel warriors who had been resisting the Taliban regime since it took over the country in 1996. At the beginning of the war, Northern Alliance troops were armed mostly with aging Russian rifles, tanks, and helicopters left over from the Soviet invasion of Afghanistan. One of the first jobs for the Green Berets in Afghanistan was to teach the Northern Alliance troops modern military tactics and how to use the latest weapons. On November 9, 2001, an A-Team along with Northern Alliance troops captured the northern Afghanistan city of Mazār-e Sharīf. It was the first major defeat for the Taliban and it set the stage for the regime's eventual collapse. By December 2001, Kandahār, the last Taliban stronghold, had fallen.

The Green Berets' job is not finished when the fighting stops. Using their language skills, A-Teams went among the

A SEAL unit discovers a cache of munitions in a cave in Zhawar Kili.

Afghan people, talking to them about the damage done by the war and discussing plans for rebuilding the country. Another daunting task was to build the fighters of the Northern Alliance, who come from many different tribes, into a cohesive national army to assure the future security of Afghanistan. "This is one of our core missions, and it's really a privilege to be involved,"[67] commented Green Beret lieutenant colonel Kevin Mc-Donnell. And it is a tangible expression of the motto of the Green Berets, *De Opresso Liber:* To Free the Oppressed.

In addition to the Rangers and Green Berets, special forces from other branches of the service also saw action in Afghanistan, including the famed U.S. Navy SEALS.

Sea, Air, and Land

Zhawar Kili is a rugged, mountainous region in eastern Afghanistan, just inside the country's border with Pakistan. Known as the location of an al-Qaeda command center and training complex, Zhawar Kili was believed to be a likely hideout for Osama bin Laden. In January 2002 a force of special-operations commandos raided the Zhawar Kili complex in an operation that was planned to take twelve hours but lasted eight days. They searched more than seventy caves and scores of aboveground buildings, only to find that their inhabitants had fled. But they discovered stores of weapons, ammunition, vehicles, and other terrorist equipment, as well as living quarters, classrooms, and offices. The commandos collected intelligence, then detonated explosives and called in air strikes to destroy the complex. Although Zhawar Kili is hundreds of miles from the nearest body of water, the successful raid was spearheaded by the navy's elite special forces warriors: the SEALs.

The U.S. Navy SEALs (SEa, Air, Land) trace their existence to the navy's Construction Battalions (CBs, or "Seabees") during World War II. In 1943 volunteer Seabees formed teams called Navy Combat Demolition Units, which were assigned to pave the way for amphibious landings by clearing obstructions on the landing beaches. During the Korean War these skilled units, renamed Underwater Demolition Teams (UDTs), conducted demolition raids on military targets, such as roads and bridges in coastal areas, and performed inland reconnaissance as well. The first SEAL teams, using personnel from UDT units, were commissioned in 1962, and in 1983 all UDT units were renamed SEAL teams. Today there are about twenty-three hundred SEALs in the navy. Their mission is to wage unconventional warfare anywhere in the world.

Training to be a SEAL is every bit as rigorous as training for other special-operations forces, with the added challenge of extensive water operations. Called Basic Underwater Demolition/SEAL, the SEAL training course is conducted at the Naval Special Warfare Center in Coronado, California. Lasting twenty-five weeks, the course is divided into three phases. Phase One takes the candidate through basic physical conditioning, which includes running, swimming, and negotiating obstacle courses. An indication of the difficulty of this phase is the so-called hell week, where trainees spend five days in continuous training with only four hours of sleep for the entire period. Phase Two covers underwater diving skills, and Phase Three teaches land warfare, including small-unit operations, land navigation, and demolition and weapons training. Like other special-operations forces, SEALs learn how to parachute from aircraft flying at high altitudes.

SEALs in Action

In Operation Enduring Freedom, SEAL teams served deep "in-country," operating on their own or with other coalition special forces teams. "We travel in very small elements," recounts a veteran SEAL, "somewhere between seven [and] fourteen people. Usually we have a 14-man platoon with two officers assigned to it. We have two, seven-man fire teams. . . . We dress just like the people in the country we go to. If it requires growing a beard, dying our hair, we do it. We send in guys who speak the language fluently."[68] SEALs performed reconnaissance missions, scouted out a small airfield that would become the U.S. operating base called Camp Rhino, and searched caves and bunkers for Taliban troops and the terrorist leaders of al-Qaeda. Besides the Zhawar Kili raid, SEALs helped capture Mullah Kahirkhawa, a Taliban leader, searched ships for contraband and al-Qaeda terrorists, and participated in the battle at Takur Ghar during Operation Anaconda that took the life of one of their members.

While army and navy special-operations forces were carrying out their quiet missions in Afghanistan, the U.S. Air Force Special Operations Command was also doing its part in the war on terrorism.

Air Commandos

Established in 1990, the Air Force Special Operations Command (AFSOC) deploys highly specialized air force personnel on high-risk assignments around the world. The roots of the AFSOC go back to World War II and an elite unit of air warriors created by army air force general Henry H. "Hap" Arnold. These "air commandos" flew dangerous missions against both Germany and Japan, inserting agents into enemy territory, rescuing wounded soldiers, and staging hit-and-run attacks. In 1961 the air force, now a separate military branch, created a new unit as a "self sufficient, self-contained force that could deploy anywhere in the world and conduct operations."[69] By the time Operation Enduring Freedom began, the AFSOC had approximately 12,500

A SEAL observes as his team destroys enemy munitions in eastern Afghanistan.

"Who Dares Wins"

Along with the many American special forces units fighting in Afghanistan, Great Britain also sent special forces troops to fight terrorism in Operation Enduring Freedom. These soldiers wear the tan beret of the elite British Special Air Service, known as the SAS.

The creation of a small, highly mobile special forces unit was the idea of a World War II Scottish officer named David Stirling. In 1941 Stirling organized a force of highly motivated soldiers to undertake operations behind enemy lines. Their first mission in November 1941 ended in disaster, with only one-third of Stirling's men returning safely. Since that inauspicious beginning, the SAS has become one of the world's premier special-operations forces, seeing action in such exotic locales as Malaya,

Borneo, and Oman. In the 1970s the SAS developed counterterrorist capabilities, allowing rapid response to terrorist kidnappings and hijackings. In 1980 the SAS ended a terrorist siege at the Iranian embassy in London, a success that brought them international fame.

The SAS has four active squadrons, each divided into four sixteen-man troops: Air Troop, Boat Troop, Mountain Troop, and Mobility Troop. Each SAS soldier specializes in one of these areas, but acquires skills in the other three disciplines as well. Counterterrorism training is also required of all SAS personnel. In Afghanistan, as well as in other hot spots around the world, the SAS has proved the truth of its motto, "Who Dares Wins."

airmen and support personnel ready, as their motto states, to go "Anywhere, Anytime."

Headquartered at Hurlbut Field in Florida, the AFSOC includes the Sixteenth Special Operations Wing, which flies such aircraft as the AC-130 "Spectre" and "Spooky" gunships, E-C-130 Commando Solo aircraft, and the MH-53 Pave Low helicopter. Also at Hurlbut, the 720th Special Tactics Group specializes in such operations as mounting rescue missions for downed fliers or other wounded personnel, weather forecasting, and deploying combat controllers into hazardous areas. "We are the Air Force's only ground combat force," commented Captain Mike Martin, chief of operations for the 720th. "There are some base ground defense units, but we go forward." [70]

Going forward means inserting combat control teams (CCTs) into a combat zone or other hostile environment. These teams pro-

vide air traffic control and communication, direct fire from aircraft onto enemy targets, survey areas for landing zones, and clear obstacles from those zones. CCTs are also experts in demolition techniques and weapons systems, parachuting, SCUBA diving, and using lasers to mark enemy targets. Transportation on the ground can mean using all-terrain vehicles, motorcycles, or amphibious vehicles.

During Operation Enduring Freedom the AFSOC contributed greatly to the war on terrorism. Secretary of the Air Force James G. Roche recounted the AFSOC successes in a speech to a group of air commandos:

You've surveyed, opened and controlled 15 austere airfields and six lakebed-landing zones. You've successfully executed more than 630 terminal air strikes resulting in 2.2 million pounds of munitions on target. You've flown more than 17,000 hours and more than 3,600 sorties in support of operations. You've provided support for more than 8,000 missions, including unconventional warfare, special reconnaissance, direct action, airfield operations and combat search and rescue.[71]

What makes a special forces soldier special? According to Command Chief Master Sergeant Bob Martens of the AFSOC, "They're really just ordinary people, but they're doing extraordinary things, day in and day out."[72] In order to do those extraordinary things, however, they need exceptional tools. Fortunately, the United States has developed the most advanced weapons in the world, and they were available to the special forces troops whose mission was to be in the thick of the fighting in Afghanistan.

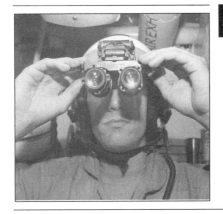

Chapter 7

Ground War Weapons

Many of the kinds of weapons used by individual soldiers on the ground in Afghanistan and other fields of battle in the war on terrorism might seem familiar to a warrior of long ago. Firearms that must be loaded and aimed, handheld explosives that are thrown at an enemy, and protective body armor have long been standard tools of the infantry soldier's trade. There the comparison ends, however; the accuracy, reliability, and deadliness of today's weapons and the protection afforded by revolutionary new materials are unprecedented and would astonish any soldier of an earlier era. A medieval knight encased in a heavy suit of armor would marvel at a lightweight Kevlar vest, and even the World War II GI with his M1 Garand rifle would be amazed by the lethal efficiency of the modern M4 carbine. The U.S. military brings to the war on terrorism the best equipped, most technologically advanced soldiers in history.

Small Arms

The long-barreled firearm has been a basic weapon of the foot soldier since its invention in Europe around the fourteenth century. Originating as simply a long tube into which a projectile and gunpowder were inserted, this relatively primitive weapon had a rod or stick that supported it from the ground. In time a wooden stock was added, allowing the soldier to brace the weapon with his shoulder. Through the years, advances were made in gun design and in the method of igniting the gunpowder. By the early 1600s the flintlock, in which a piece of flint created a spark to fire the gun, was invented; it would remain a standard military weapon for more than two centuries.

Around the year 1500 an improvement known as "rifling" was added to long-barreled weapons. A series of spiral grooves cut into the inside of the gun's barrel, rifling spins the bullet to increase its range and accuracy. Rifles have played a major role in American history. The Springfield rifle was used extensively by Union soldiers during the Civil War, and a Confederate version was manufactured in the South. World War II soldiers used the M1 Garand rifle, a weapon that held eight rounds, or bullets, in a replaceable clip. During the 1960s the standard U.S. military rifle was the M-16. Manufactured by the Colt Firearms Company for use in the Vietnam War, hundreds of thousands of M-16s were brought to the conflict in Southeast Asia by U.S. troops. It was a formidable weapon that could accurately fire 700 to 950 rounds per minute with a range of up to 1,300 feet.

The M-16 was not without its problems, however. In the hot and humid jungles of Vietnam it tended to jam and required frequent cleaning, a task not easily performed in a combat zone. And it lacked one of the most basic parts of a rifle: a shoulder sling. Despite its problems the M-16 became the standard weapon of the U.S. military. But

U.S. soldiers march with M-16 rifles during a 1966 mission in Vietnam.

as special-operations activities increased during and after the Cold War, it was determined that a new, more versatile weapon was needed. When special forces troops entered Afghanistan they brought with them an improved version of the M-16, the M4A1.

Special-Ops Weapons

In 1994 a new weapon, based on the M-16 but lighter and more compact, was adopted by the U.S. Army. Called the M4 carbine (a carbine is any rifle shortened for ease of handling or for use in close quarters), this rifle shares about 80 percent of its parts with the M-16. The M4 uses 5.56 mm rounds and can fire short bursts of three rounds per trigger pull. Weighing five and a half pounds and measuring about thirty inches long, the M4 carbine is accurate up to nineteen hundred feet. Although already a highly effective weapon, the M4 needed further modification to meet the demands of

The M4 carbine, an improved version of the M-16, is a compact, highly accurate rifle.

Explosives for Commandos

Among the weaponry that a special forces soldier must be familiar with are those tools of combat that "go bang": explosives such as hand grenades and mines. Such weapons include the following explosive devices, as compiled from the Federation of American Scientists website:

> M67 fragmentation grenade: This fourteen-ounce sphere is filled with six and a half ounces of explosive called Composition B. When detonated the M67's charge shatters the grenade's steel body into small, jagged shrapnel that can kill within fifteen feet and injure anyone within a radius of almost fifty feet.

> M18 colored smoke grenade: While not a lethal weapon, the M18 is used as a signaling device to mark targets or landing zones. The cylindrical grenade contains a filler that, when ignited, releases colored smoke (red, yellow, green, or purple) for up to ninety seconds. In addition to signaling, the M18 can provide a smoke screen to obscure troop movements.

> MK3A2 concussion grenade: This grenade is used when it is desirable to protect friendly troops from injury in close combat situations. It does not fragment on detonation, but produces casualties by shock waves; it is especially effective in enclosed areas such as caves or buildings.

> M18A1 Claymore mine: A directional fragmentation antipersonnel mine, the Claymore is an eight-inch by three-inch rectangular box filled with seven hundred steel pellets embedded in C-4 explosive. Placed on the ground on small legs, the mine is aimed at an enemy position. When detonated, the pellets are projected in a 60-degree horizontal arc, lethal to enemy troops within 150 feet.

special forces. "The whole intent," comments Captain William Smith of U.S. Army Special Operations, "was to make this weapon more effective from close range to extended ranges. These changes will increase its operational effectiveness through improved target recognition, acquisition and hit quality during day and night." [73] The special-operations version of the M4, called the M4A1, includes a collapsible stock and a special rail system to allow mounting of various accessories. These attachments include laser and infrared markers to pinpoint targets, a high-intensity light, and various scopes and sights to customize the weapon for specific missions. The M4A1 also has automatic-fire capability that allows continuous firing as long as the trigger is pressed. This new weapon, actually a weapons system, is used by Rangers and special forces troops, as well as by air crews in special-ops aviation units.

For more firepower special forces can use the M-249 squad automatic weapon (SAW), a light machine gun that began service with the Army in 1982. It was developed to fill the gap left by the World War II–era Browning automatic rifle, which had been discontinued in the 1950s. Capable of delivering up to nine hundred 5.56 mm rounds per minute, the SAW is fed from a two-hundred-round ammunition belt or from M-16 magazines. The M-249 can be fired from many positions, including the shoulder and hip, and also from a prone position using a bipod to support the barrel. It is a rugged weapon that will operate in almost any condition or climate and will even fire after immersion in water.

The soldier on the ground in Afghanistan had other weapons at his disposal for fighting the elusive al-Qaeda and Taliban forces. Fragmentation and incendiary grenades were used to kill enemy troops who were either in the open or hiding in caves, while smoke grenades marked landing areas and pinpointed troop positions with various colored smoke. The M-9 Beretta 9 mm pistol, a lightweight semiautomatic sidearm with a fifteen-round magazine, was carried for close-in personal defense. Small and easily concealable, the M-9 was ideal for special forces missions. It replaced the famous M-1911 .45 caliber pistol that had been the standard U.S. Army sidearm since before World War I.

The weapons carried by each soldier provided enough offensive firepower to defeat the enemy in almost any situation. But when the enemy began firing back, personal protective devices became the soldier's best friend.

Modern Armor

Personal protection has been worn by warriors since medieval times, when armor-clad knights did battle with swords and lances. Until recently, however, modern protective gear was either nonexistent or too cumbersome to be practical. But all that changed with the introduction of the personnel armor system, ground troop (PASGT). This system provides a soldier with two important protective items: an armored vest and a helmet. One of the most basic items of protective gear worn by a combat soldier is the helmet. The familiar "steel pot" helmets of World War II afforded troops some protection from shrapnel and glancing blows from bullets, but they could not stop a direct hit. The PASGT helmet is the new standard military helmet. More closely resembling a German World War II helmet than the old U.S. steel model, the PASGT helmet is constructed of several layers of Kevlar, a dense, high-strength fabric. It weighs between three and four pounds, a bit more than the old helmet, but its protective qualities are superior. It provides protection for the soldier's head, ear, and neck areas, and can withstand a direct hit from a 9 mm round. Cloth covers in several camouflage patterns are available depending on the part of the world where the helmet is used.

The PASGT protective vest consists of thirteen layers of Kevlar under a water-resistant, camouflage-patterned cloth cover. It protects the front, sides, and back of the wearer's torso from fragments and shrapnel, the main source of serious combat wounds. It is estimated that if the PASGT system had been available during the Vietnam War, casualties could have been reduced by some 40 percent. The PASGT vest can be upgraded with additional armor to provide protection from direct bullet impacts, but such improvements come with a corresponding increase in weight and bulk.

Kevlar—The Fabric That Saves Lives

Of the two thousand U.S. soldiers who took part in Operation Anaconda in March 2002 only seventy-six were wounded. And of those wounds, most were not in the torso where damage to vital organs can cause serious injury or even death. Those soldiers lived because they were wearing body armor made of a remarkable fabric known as Kevlar. And they have Stephanie Kwolek to thank for it.

Stephanie Kwolek was a chemist at a time when few women pursued careers in scientific research. She began her career in 1946 at the DuPont Corporation, where she started experimenting with polymers, a special kind of chemical compound used to make such material as nylon, Dacron, and Lycra. In 1964 she discovered high-performance liquid crystal polymers that could be spun into threads like spiders spin webs. She noted that the resulting fibers were extremely strong. "Unlike ordinary nylon," Kwolek recalled for the winter 2003 issue of *Invention and Technology* magazine, "this fiber was very difficult to break by hand. At that moment I knew we had a most unusual fiber. . . . This discovery opened up a whole new field of polymer chemistry." And it led to the development of Kevlar protective armor.

When these tough fibers, which were given the name Kevlar, are woven together they create a strong fabric that is flameproof, resistant to chemicals, and can withstand blows from bullets, shrapnel, and knives. Kevlar is five times stronger than an equal weight of steel. In addition, Kevlar is flexible and lightweight, unlike previous body armor which, being heavy and uncomfortable, was often left behind by soldiers going into battle. Body armor is made up of as many as thirteen layers of Kevlar. When a Kevlar vest is hit by a bullet or shrapnel, some layers may be penetrated, but the energy of the projectile is dissipated by the rest of the layers deforming, or bending. The wearer may be bruised, but he will be alive.

Since the early 1970s DuPont has been mass-producing Kevlar for use by law enforcement agents, corrections officers, and military personnel. Kevlar is used in many other applications as well, including ropes for mooring U.S. Navy ships, jet engine shielding to protect passengers in case of an explosion, cut-resistant gloves for industry, and automobile tires that can be driven on even when flat. Its most important application, however, will always be to protect the men and women who maintain public safety and safeguard our national security.

Stephanie Kwolek was inducted into the National Inventors Hall of Fame in 1995 and was awarded the National Medal of Technology the following year. But her lasting legacy will be the countless lives saved by her invention of Kevlar.

Goggles and Lasers

With many ground missions in Operation Enduring Freedom taking place at night, troops needed help in spotting the enemy in the dark. Night-vision goggles (NVGs) provide a soldier with the ability to see and engage the enemy in nearly total darkness. "Clearly night-vision technology is essential," commented a defense specialist at the Brookings Institution, a public policy research organization. "It's one of the real trump cards we have in the battle with al-Qaeda."[74] The AN/PVS-7 NVGs can be carried by an individual soldier or attached to his helmet. Inside the unit is an image intensifier tube that amplifies the faintest light from stars or other ambient sources up to fifty thousand times. Looking into the binocular eyepieces the soldier sees the scene displayed, in shades of green, as clearly as if it were daylight. For use on nights when there is no ambient light at all, an infrared

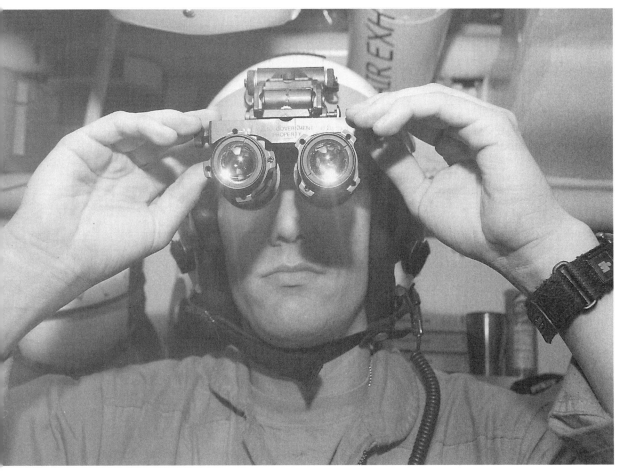

A pilot adjusts his night-vision goggles in preparation for a mission.

illuminator lights up the scene with infrared light that is invisible to the naked eye but can be seen by the AN/PVS-7.

The AN/PVS-7 weighs just over one pound and can operate for up to forty hours on batteries. All special forces troops are issued NVGs, and pilots of fixed- and rotary-wing aircraft also use them for night flying. And while al-Qaeda and the Taliban may have had some night-vision equipment, it clearly did not impair the U.S. mission to defeat the terrorists in Afghanistan.

Lasers too have become an indispensable part of modern battlefield equipment. That equipment includes laser range finders and target designators. Lasers (the name is an acronym for "light amplification by stimulated emission of radiation") produce a very bright, highly concentrated beam of light. A laser range finder measures the distance to a target by emitting a short burst of laser light. When it hits the target, some of that light is reflected. The range finder measures the time it takes for the reflection to return and calculates how far away the target is, giving the operator the precise distance to the enemy.

Another important use for battlefield lasers is "terminal guidance," or marking target positions for laser-guided munitions such as Bunker-Buster bombs or Maverick missiles. For this job an enhanced laser range finder called a laser target designator (LTD) is used. The operator aims the designator at the target during the munition's terminal phase, or last few seconds, of its flight. Unlike the laser range finder's brief burst, the LTD fires a continuous laser beam. The reflected beam is picked up by sensors in the bomb or missile and guides it to an accurate impact on the target. By pulsing the laser, the beam is coded so that only a bomb programmed with that same code will hit the target. This assures that the bomb will hit only its designated target and allows many weapons to operate simultaneously without getting "confused" by multiple laser beams flashing around the battlefield. The LTD is not foolproof, however, with deadly consequences. In December 2001 near Kandahār, three Green Berets and five Afghans were killed by a U.S. two-thousand-pound bomb. The error occurred when one of the Green Berets, who was relaying target coordinates to bombers flying high above, replaced dead batteries in his LTD. He did not realize that unless he reentered the target's

position the device automatically began transmitting its own coordinates, thus calling down the bomb on the Green Berets and their Afghan comrades.

The AN/PEQ-1A special-operations forces laser marker (SOFLAM) is a portable laser range finder/target designator used by army Rangers and special forces, navy SEALs and air force special-ops units. Weighing just twelve pounds, the battery-powered SOFLAM can be carried and operated by one soldier. Supported by a tripod or any other sturdy base such as a vehicle or even a large rock, it can mark a target more than three miles away. A night-vision scope can be attached to the SOFLAM, making it useful not only in daylight but also at night and in other low-light situations.

The advanced weapons used in Operation Enduring Freedom seemed miraculous to some less sophisticated Afghan warriors fighting alongside U.S. special forces. For example, one special forces captain describes a bit of battlefield deception that left the impression that the laser target designator was a "death ray":

> If you timed it just right, as the laser target designator is engaging and [targeting the] enemy position, you let your Northern Alliance commander take a look through the laser target designator. He sees it going, but he doesn't see the bombs fly into the target. He hears that chirping noise from the laser target designator and then the enemy position explodes. They believe

that we have the death ray, and this was a myth that we were willing to perpetuate. . . . This whole situation is like the Flintstones meet the Jetsons. And those guys could not fathom that we have some sort of aiming device that would allow us to hit a target at night on the first round. [75]

One of the most dangerous jobs of ground troops during Operation Enduring Freedom was searching Afghanistan's seem-

Riding into Battle

Horses have been an essential part of warfare from ancient times. As late as World War I horses were transporting troops, dragging guns and ammunition wagons into battle, and saving lives by pulling ambulances. In twenty-first century military operations, however, with supersonic jets, massive aircraft carriers, and smart munitions, the use of horses in combat would seem to be a thing of the long distant past. And that is what the generals thought until the United States went to war in Afghanistan. The following is a portion of an address given by Secretary of Defense Donald Rumsfeld at the National Defense University on January 31, 2002. The entire speech can be found at the DefenseLink website (www. defenselink.mil).

Among the many [soldiers] I met was an extraordinary group of men—the Special Forces who had been involved in the attack on Mazar-i-Sharif. Now, I have said on many occasions that the war on terrorism would be unlike any war that had been fought before. These men surprised us all with one of their early requests for supplies. They asked for boots, ammunition . . . and horse-feed.

From the moment they landed in Afghanistan, they began adapting to the circumstances on the ground. They sported beards and traditional scarves, and rode horses trained to run into machine gun fire, atop saddles fashioned from wood, and saddlebags crafted from Afghan carpets. They used pack-mules to transport equipment across some of the roughest terrain in the world, riding at night, in darkness, near minefields and along narrow mountain trails with drops so sheer that, as one soldier put it "it took me a week to ease the death-grip on my horse." Many had never been on horseback before.

As they linked up and trained with anti-Taliban forces, they learned from their new allies about the realities of war on Afghan soil—and assisted them with weapons, food, supplies, tactics, training, and know-how. And they planned the assault on Mazar.

On the appointed day, one of their teams slipped in and hid well behind enemy lines—ready to call in the air strikes. The bomb blasts would be the signal for the others to charge. When the moment came, they signaled their targets to coalition aircraft . . . and looked at their watches. "Two minutes." "Thirty seconds." "Fifteen seconds." Then, out of nowhere, a hail of precision-guided bombs began to land on Taliban and al Qaeda positions. The explosions were deafening—and the timing was so precise that, as the soldiers described it, hundreds of Afghan horsemen emerged, literally, out of the smoke, riding down on the enemy through clouds of dust and flying shrapnel. A few carried RPGs [rocket-propelled grenades], some had less than ten rounds of ammunition in their guns—but they rode boldly—Americans and Afghans—into tank, mortar, artillery and sniper fire.

It was the first U.S. cavalry battle of the 21st Century.

The PackBot robot can navigate virtually any terrain. The army used the PackBot to search the Taliban's cave hideouts.

ingly endless caves to root out Taliban and al-Qaeda soldiers who may have taken refuge there. Yet some troops sent into these dark and dangerous caverns were unfazed by the unknown hazards within. They approached their mission with steely resolve and a complete lack of fear. Indeed, these warriors were incapable of fear, for they were robots.

Mechanical Warriors

The robots of Operation Enduring Freedom did not look much like the androids depicted in science fiction movies: no legs, no arms, not even a head. But with their TV-camera eyes and computer-chip brains they were able to replace their human comrades in many hazardous situations. The soldiers gave them nicknames like Fester, Hermes, and Thing, but the robots were officially known as Pack-Bots, and their use in Afghanistan heralded a new age of warfare. "This is history," says Colonel Bruce Jette, head of the army's ro-

botics team. "Nobody has ever used a robot in combat before." [76]

The PackBot is a low, flat "bot" about the size of a suitcase: sixteen inches wide, twenty-seven inches long, and only seven inches high. It moves on tanklike treads that can propel it at more than eight miles per hour in its high-speed mode. Tracked "flippers" mounted on the front wheels allow PackBot to navigate rough terrain, mounting hills and even climbing up stairs. It weighs forty pounds and thus is portable enough to be carried by an individual soldier in a backpack. But as small as it is, Pack-Bot is also extremely rugged. It can withstand a shock of four hundred times the force of gravity and will operate nearly ten feet underwater. In addition, PackBot is smart. It has a Pentium computer brain, a Global Positioning System receiver, a communication system for remote operation, and inputs for up to twelve video sources. Each PackBot costs around forty-five thousand dollars and is built from readily available, off-the-shelf parts.

PackBot's designers envisioned many different jobs for the little robot besides remote surveillance, including delivering ammunition or medical supplies to troops in a battle zone, detecting biological or radiation hazards, searching for unexploded land mines, or inspecting damaged buildings. This last capability was put to the test shortly after September 11, 2001, when PackBot joined several other robots in surveying the damage at the World Trade Center site. But this was not PackBot's last mission in the fight against terror. "The same robot that helped with the recovery effort at the World Trade Center," noted Tom Frost, a technical manager for the robot's manufacturer, "is now in Afghanistan trying to track down the people that did it." [77]

Searching the Caves

The PackBot began its slow journey toward a cave located in a complex of about a dozen similar caverns in the rugged region of eastern Afghanistan. Its treads grinding along the dusty ground of a dry riverbed, the small robot picked its way over potential obstacles such as rocks with its mechanical flippers. Searching the caves of Afghanistan was an extremely hazardous mission, for they had been used as hideouts

for the Taliban and al-Qaeda. By July 2002, with the Taliban out of power and al-Qaeda scattered, the caves remained dangerous places. While their occupants may or may not still be hiding there, mines and booby traps could lie in wait for the unsuspecting soldier. Exploring this hazardous environment was a job tailor-made for PackBot.

The mission to use a robot to explore these caves fell to the army's Eighty-Second Airborne Division. A group of these soldiers watched as one of their members guided PackBot into the cave's opening with a computerized remote control unit he wore on his battle fatigues. Once inside the cave, PackBot's TV-camera eyes surveyed the interior and transmitted the pictures back to the soldiers waiting safely outside. "I don't have to be anywhere near this cave," said one of PackBot's human comrades. "By looking through [an] eyepiece I . . . can switch cameras so I can see exactly what I need to see." [78] What he does not see is a Taliban or al-Qaeda terrorist—the cave is empty. And since PackBot has not triggered any mines or other booby traps, the cave is considered safe for the soldiers to enter. Mission accomplished with no casualties—either human or robot.

Avoiding casualties is, of course, a major incentive for using robots such as PackBot in combat. And while losing a forty-five-thousand-dollar robot to a mine or bomb might be expensive, it is without question preferable to losing a human life. As Colonel Jette summed it up, "I don't have any problem writing to [the manufacturer] and saying 'I'm sorry your robot died, can we get another?' That's a lot easier letter to write than [one] to a father or mother."[79]

The Weapons of Future Wars

Many new "robosoldiers" are being developed by manufacturers who envision a day when wars may be fought without a human soldier ever setting foot on the battlefield. The exotic robots range from small "throwable microbots" that can be tossed into an enemy building, to parachute-dropped "mother robots" that release a payload of armed "munition-bots" for search-and-destroy missions. Even little PackBot may one day be armed with shotguns or grenade launchers.

Robots, unmanned aerial vehicles, Bunker-Buster bombs, spy satellites, and laser-guided missiles all played a part in the success of Operation Enduring Freedom. But as impressive as all this advanced weaponry is, it still takes the human mind and human hands to design, build, and test these marvels of modern technology. And it takes people, the men and women of the United States armed forces, to ultimately use these weapons in combat. If a robot can keep our soldiers safer, if a laser-targeted missile can prevent civilian casualties, if all these weapons can somehow make warfare just a little less devastating, then they will serve their purpose in wars to come. For all their technological wonders, however, there is one thing that modern weapons cannot do: They cannot predict a surprise attack on America like the one that occurred on September 11, 2001. Perhaps the existence of these weapons can deter future terrorist aggression; but their military effectiveness means U.S. soldiers, sailors, airmen, and marines will go into combat in the war on terrorism equipped with the most advanced weapons in the world.

☆ Notes ☆

Introduction: "How Will We Fight and Win This War?"

1. Quoted in White House, "Address to a Joint Session of Congress and the American People." www.whitehouse.gov.
2. Quoted in White House, "Address to a Joint Session of Congress and the American People."

Chapter 1: Organizing for Battle

3. Quoted in Jeffrey Bartholet, Owen Matthews, and Roy Gutman, "Rising Above the Ruins," *Newsweek*, October 8, 2001, p. 40.
4. Quoted in White House, "Address to a Joint Session of Congress and the American People."
5. Quoted in Global Security, *Operation Enduring Freedom*. www.globalsecurity.org.
6. Quoted in PBS, "Campaign Against Terror," *Frontline*. www.pbs org.
7. Milan Vego, "What Can We Learn From Enduring Freedom?" *Proceedings*, July 2002, p. 28.
8. U.S. Navy Office of Information, ". . . From the Sea: Preparing the Naval Service for the 21st Century." www.chinfo.navy.mil.
9. Quoted in Global Security, "Where Are the Carriers?" www.globalsecurity.org.

10. Tom Clancy, *Carrier: A Guided Tour of an Aircraft Carrier.* New York: Berkley, 1999, p. 200.
11. Tom Clancy, *Carrier,* p. 226.
12. Quoted in Melissa Martinez, "*Carl Vinson* Sailors Return Home as Heroes," USS *Carl Vinson* press release, CVN-70, January 23, 2002. www.cvn70.navy.mil.

Chapter 2: Air Attack over Afghanistan

13. Quoted in Robert Wall, "Navy Adapts Operations for Afghan War Hurdles," *Aviation Week and Space Technology,* Aviation Now, November 19, 2001. www.aviation now.com.
14. Quoted in Orr Kelly, *Hornet: The Inside Story of the F/A-18.* Novato, CA: Presidio, 1990, p. 81.
15. Quoted in Kelly, *Hornet,* p. 87.
16. Quoted in Frank Pelligrini, "What in the World Is Diego Garcia?" *Time.* www.time.com.
17. Quoted in Louis A. Arana-Barradas, "Bomber Strikes from Diego Garcia a Fifteen-Hour Ordeal," AirForceLink. www.af.mil.
18. Quoted in Arana-Barradas, "Bomber Strikes from Diego Garcia a Fifteen-Hour Ordeal."

19. Quoted in Steve Pace, *B-2 Spirit: The Most Capable War Machine on the Planet.* New York: McGraw-Hill, 2000, p. 79.

20. Quoted in DefenseLink, Department of Defense news briefing, October 16, 2001. www.defenselink.mil.

21. Quoted in Paul Richter, "U.S. Gunship Offers Awesome Firepower," *Los Angeles Times,* October 17, 2001, Global Security. www.globalsecurity.org.

Chapter 3: Bombs and Missiles

22. Quoted in DefenseLink, Department of Defense news briefing, November 28, 2001. www.defenselink.mil.

23. Quoted in DefenseLink, Department of Defense news briefing, November 1, 2001. www.defenselink.mil.

24. David Williams, "Pulverised by the Daisy Cutter," *War on Terror,* Associated News Media. www.femail.co.uk.

25. Williams, "Pulverised by the Daisy Cutter."

26. Federation of American Scientists, "Reaching Globally, Reaching Powerfully: The United States of Air Force in the Gulf War. A Report—September 1991." www.fas.org.

27. Quoted in Patrick J. Sloyan, "The Bargain Basement Bomb," *Long Island Newsday,* November 14, 1999, p. 23.

28. Quoted in Paul Weisman, "Afghanistan Caves Thwart Invaders." *USA Today,* November 5, 2001. www.usatoday.com.

29. Quoted in Kris Osborn, "Air Force Seeks Deeper-Penetrating 'Bunker-Busters,'" CNN. www.cnn.com.

30. Quoted in CNN, "Pentagon to Use New Bomb on Afghan Caves." www.cnn.com.

31. Quoted in Kathleen T. Rehm, "Fliers Share Enduring Freedom Experiences at Andrews Open House," DC Military. www.dcmilitary.com.

32. Quoted in John B. Nathman, "'We Were Great': Navy Air in Afghanistan," *Proceedings,* U.S. Naval Institute, March 2002. www.usni.org.

Chapter 4: Support Aircraft and Helicopters

33. Quoted in Terry Joyce, "Airmen Mark Milestone in Humanitarian Effort," *Charleston Post and Courier.* http://archives.charleston.net.

34. Quoted in Dani Johnson, "A Look Back at OEF HUMRO—The Operation," U.S. Air Force Air Mobility Command. https://amcpublic.scott.af.mil.

35. Quoted in Johnson, "A Look Back at OEF HUMRO—The Operation."

36. Quoted in Johnson, "A Look Back at OEF HUMRO—The Operation."

37. Quoted in Federation of American Scientists, "Commando Solo: EC130 Crew Targets Message to Battlefield, Troubled Country." www.fas.org.

38. Quoted in Jim Garamone, "U.S. Commando Solo II Takes Over Afghan Airwaves," American Forces Press Service, Clandestine Radio. www.clandestineradio.com.

39. Quoted in Steve Vogel, "Gas Stations in the Sky Extend Fighters' Reach." *Washington Post,* November 1, 2001. www.washingtonpost.com.

40. Lexington Institute, "Killing Al Qaeda: The Navy's Role," Naval Strike Forum White Paper, March 2002. www.lexington institute.org.

41. Quoted in Sean D. Naylor, "In Shah-E-Kot, Apaches Save the Day—and Their Reputation," *Army Times,* 21st Cavalry Brigade (Air Combat). www.hood.army.mil.

42. Quoted in Linda D. Kozaryn, "Chinooks Triumph over Afghan Conditions," *Tandem Notes,* vol. 9, no. 3, Boeing. www.boeing.com.

Chapter 5: Gathering Intelligence

43. Quoted in Norman Polmar and Thomas B. Allen, *Spy Book: The Encyclopedia of Espionage.* New York: Random House, 1997, p. 541.

44. Quoted in Robert Roy Britt, "Satellites Play Crucial Roles in Air and Ground Battles," Space.com. www.space.com.

45. Quoted in Bijal P. Trivedi, "U.S. Buys Up Afghanistan Images from Top Satellite," *National Geographic Today,* October 25, 2001. http://news.national geographic.com.

46. Quoted in Trivedi, "U.S. Buys Up Afghanistan Images from Top Satellite."

47. Quoted in Britt, "Satellites Play Crucial Roles in Air and Ground Battles."

48. Quoted in Jim Garamone, "Flying an Unmanned Aerial Vehicle," American Forces Press Service, DefenseLink, April 23, 2002. www.defenselink.mil.

49. Quoted in Terrorism Project, *International Herald Tribune,* December 28, 2001. www.cdi.org.

50. Quoted in Jim Garamone, "Unmanned Aerial Vehicles Proving Their Worth Over Afghanistan," American Forces Press Service, DefenseLink, April 16, 2002. www.defenselink.mil.

51. Thomas E. Ricks, "U.S. Arms Unmanned Aircraft," *Washington Post,* SouthCoast Today, October 17, 2001. www.s-t.com.

52. Judith Miller and Eric Schmitt, "A Nation Challenged: Ugly Duckling Turns Out to Be Formidable in the Air," *New York Times,* November 23, 2001, Terrorism Project. www.cdi.org.

53. Quoted in John McWethy, "Robo-Planes: Unmanned Aircraft Redefines How Military Wages War," ABC News. http://abc news.go.com.

54. Quoted in McWethy, "Robo-Planes."

55. Quoted in William Speed Weed, "Flying Blind," *Discover,* August 2002, p. 60.

56. Quoted in Weed, "Flying Blind," p. 60.

57. Quoted in DefenseLink, Department of Defense news briefing, November 2, 2001. www.defenselink.mil.

Chapter 6: Special-Operations Forces

58. DefenseLink, Department of Defense news briefing, October 20, 2001. www. defenselink.mil.

59. Quoted in Tanya Biank, "Lt. Gen. Brown Shares War Stories," *Fayetteville (NC) Observer,* U.S. Army Special Forces, June 29, 2002. www.groups.sfahq.com.

60. Quoted in John Barry and Arian Campo-Flores, "The Warriors of the Night," *Newsweek,* October 29, 2001, pp. 25, 27.

61. DefenseLink, Department of Defense news briefing, October 20, 2001.

62. DefenseLink, Department of Defense news briefing, October 20, 2001.

63. Tom Clancy with John Gresham, *Special Forces: A Guided Tour of U.S. Army Special Forces.* New York: Berkley, 2001, p. 70.

64. Quoted in Barry and Campo-Flores, "The Warriors of the Night," p. 28.

65. Quoted in Kirk Spitzer, "Green Berets Outfought, Outthought the Taliban," *USA Today,* January 6, 2002. www.usa today.com.

66. DefenseLink, Department of Defense news briefing, October 7, 2001. www. defenselink.mil.

67. Quoted in Charles Portman, "Green Berets Standing Up Afghan Army," Army-Link. www.dtic.mil.

68. Quoted in Kris Osborn, "Navy Seals Play Crucial Role in War on Terror," CNN. www.cnn.com.

69. Quoted in Timothy Baily, "Air Commando! A Heritage Wrapped in Secrecy." *Airman,* U.S. Air Force, March 1997. www.af.mil.

70. Quoted in Scott Gourley, "Air Force Special Ops," *Popular Mechanics,* April 2002, p. 73.

71. James G. Roche, "Salute to Air Commandos," speech at Andrews Air Force Base, U.S. Air Force, October 9, 2002. www.af.mil.

72. Quoted in Gourley, "Air Force Special Ops," p. 77.

Chapter 7: Ground War Weapons

73. Quoted in Nelson Mumma Jr., "Special Operations Improves M4 Carbine," Army News Service, ArmyLink, September 14, 1998. www.dtic.mil.

74. Quoted in Amanda Onion, "Owning the Night," ABC News.com. http://abc news.go.com.

75. Quoted in PBS, "Campaign Against Terror."

76. Quoted in Tanalee Smith, "Robots Draw Rough Duty as U.S. Combat-Tests Them in Afghanistan." Associated Press, Space.com, July 30, 2002. www.space.com.

77. Quoted in David Buchbinder, "In Afghanistan, a New Robosoldier Goes to War," *Christian Science Monitor,* July 31, 2002. www.csmonitor.com.

78. Quoted in Nic Robertson, "Meet Packbot: The Newest Recruit," CNN, August 10, 2002. www.cnn.com.

79. Quoted in CNN, "Military Robots Well Trained for War," Associated Press, January 13, 2003. http://asia. cnn.com.

★ For Further Reading ★

Mark Beyer, *Aircraft Carriers Inside and Out*. New York: Power Plus, 2002. This book provides a fascinating look at the history and operation of aircraft carriers from their beginning to the present day. Illustrated with drawings, diagrams, and black-and-white and color photographs.

Robin Cross, *Modern Military Weapons*. New York: Aladdin, 1991. The weapons of land, sea, and air warfare are depicted with numerous color photographs and illustrations, but brief text. Includes a glossary.

Timothy R. Gaffney, *Secret Spy Satellites: America's Eyes in Space*. Berkeley Heights, NJ: Enslow, 2000. This book tells the story of spy satellites beginning with the Corona program, and speculates on the future of spying from outer space.

David Miller and Gerard Ridefort, *Modern Elite Forces*. New York: Smithmark Publishers, 1992. This book examines the special-warfare units of many nations and discusses their training, weapons, and missions.

Mike Spick and Barry Wheeler, *Modern American Fighters and Attack Aircraft*. New York: Smithmark, 1992. Fighters, bombers, and attack helicopters are profiled in this illustrated guide to the air arsenals of the U.S. Air Force, Army, Navy, and Marines.

George Sullivan, *Elite Warriors: The Special Forces of the United States and Its Allies*. New York: Facts On File, 1995. The author presents an in-depth look at the Rangers, Green Berets, Delta Force, and Air Force Special Forces, plus the special forces of several other nations. Illustrated with black-and-white photographs.

S.F. Tomajczyk, *Modern U.S. Navy Destroyers*. Osceola, WI: MBI, 2001. A fully illustrated guide to U.S. destroyers, including a glossary and table of destroyer data.

★ Works Consulted ★

Books

Tom Clancy, *Carrier: A Guided Tour of an Aircraft Carrier*. New York: Berkley, 1999. An in-depth look at a nuclear-powered carrier by best-selling military writer Clancy. Provides detailed information on the aircraft, weapons, and operations of this floating city. Includes photos, drawings, and diagrams, plus a glossary.

Tom Clancy with John Gresham, *Special Forces: A Guided Tour of U.S. Army Special Forces*. New York: Berkley, 2001. The authors examine the world of the Green Beret, including recruitment and training, weapons, and missions. Along with photos and drawings, the book contains an interview with the former head of Special Operations Command and a mininovel.

Orr Kelly, *Hornet: The Inside Story of the F/A-18*. Novato, CA: Presidio, 1990. A comprehensive history of the F/A-18 Hornet, the controversial but revolutionary strike fighter. Includes black-and-white photographs and drawings.

Steve Pace, *B-2 Spirit: The Most Capable War Machine on the Planet*. New York: McGraw-Hill, 2000. The inside story of the development, wartime service, and future of the revolutionary B-2 stealth bomber. Illustrated with numerous black-and-white photographs, plus a color photo section.

Norman Polmar and Thomas B. Allen, *Spy Book: The Encyclopedia of Espionage*. New York: Random House, 1997. A comprehensive encyclopedia of the "cloak-and-dagger" trades from ancient times to the present day. Twenty-seven master articles cover major themes in espionage, while other entries detail spies, their methods and equipment, and other fascinating intelligence topics.

Fred J. Pushies, *U.S. Army Special Forces*. St. Paul, MN: MBI, 2001. A readable account of the Green Berets, illustrated with numerous black-and-white and color photographs.

Periodicals

John Barry and Arian Campo-Flores, "The Warriors of the Night," *Newsweek*, October 29, 2001.

Jeffrey Bartholet, Owen Matthews, and Roy Gutman, "Rising Above the Ruins," *Newsweek*, October 8, 2001.

Scott Gourley, "Air Force Special Ops," *Popular Mechanics*, April 2002.

Jim Quinn, Hall of Fame interview by Stephanie Kwolek, *Invention and Technology*, Winter 2003.

Patrick J. Sloyan, "The Bargain Basement Bomb," *Long Island Newsday,* November 14, 1999.

Milan Vego, "What Can We Learn From Enduring Freedom?" *Proceedings,* July 2002.

William Speed Weed, "Flying Blind," *Discover,* August 2002.

Internet Sources

Louis A. Arana-Barradas, "Bomber Strikes from Diego Garcia a Fifteen-Hour Ordeal," AirForceLink. www.af.mil.

AviationToday.com, "Airborne Law Enforcement: A Different Beat," *Rotor & Wing,* July 2002. www.aviationtoday.com.

Timothy Baily, "Air Commando! A Heritage Wrapped in Secrecy," *Airman,* U.S. Air Force, March 1997. www.af.mil.

Tanya Biank, "Lt. Gen. Brown Shares War Stories," *Fayetteville (NC) Observer,* U.S. Army Special Forces, June 29, 2002. www.groups.sfahq.com.

Robert Roy Britt, "Satellites Play Crucial Roles in Air and Ground Battles," Space.com. www.space.com.

David Buchbinder, "In Afghanistan, a New Robosoldier Goes to War," *Christian Science Monitor,* July 31, 2002. www.csmonitor.com.

Duncan Campbell, "Tommy Franks: He's No Stormin' Norman," *Guardian,* November 17, 2001. www.guardian.co.uk.

CNN, "Military Robots Well Trained for War," Associated Press, January 13, 2003. http://asia.cnn.com.

———, "Pentagon to Use New Bomb on Afghan Caves." www.cnn.com.

DefenseLink, Department of Defense news briefings, October 7–November 28, 2001. www.defenselink.mil.

Federation of American Scientists, "Commando Solo: EC130 Crew Targets Message to Battlefield, Troubled Country." www.fas.org.

———, "Reaching Globally, Reaching Powerfully: The United States Air Force in the Gulf War. A Report—September 1991." www.fas.org.

Jim Garamone, "Flying an Unmanned Aerial Vehicle," American Forces Press Service, DefenseLink, April 23, 2002. www.defenselink.mil.

———, "Unmanned Aerial Vehicles Proving Their Worth Over Afghanistan," American Forces Press Service, DefenseLink, April 16, 2002. www.defenselink.mil.

———, "U.S. Commando Solo II Takes Over Afghan Airwaves," American Forces Press Service, Clandestine Radio. www.clandestineradio.com.

Global Security, *Operation Enduring Freedom.* www.globalsecurity.org.

———, "Where Are the Carriers?" www.globalsecurity.org.

Timothy Hoffman, "Air Force Bomber Tactics Enhanced by Integrated Space Systems," U.S. Air Force. www.af.mil.

Dani Johnson, "A Look Back at OEF HUMRO—The Operation," U.S. Air Force Air Mobility Command. https://amcpublic.scott.af.mil.

Terry Joyce, "Airmen Mark Milestone in Humanitarian Effort," *Charleston Post and Courier.* http://archives.charleston.net.

————, "Over Afghanistan in a C-17," *Charleston Post and Courier.* http://archives. charleston.net.

Linda D. Kozaryn, "Chinooks Triumph over Afghan Conditions," *Tandem Notes,* vol. 9, no. 3, Boeing. www.boeing.com.

Lexington Institute, "Killing Al Qaeda: The Navy's Role," Naval Strike Forum White Paper, March 2002. www.lexington institute.org.

Melissa Martinez, "*Carl Vinson* Sailors Return Home as Heroes," USS *Carl Vinson* press release, CVN-70, January 23, 2002. www.cvn70.navy.mil.

Jamie McIntyre, "U.S. Propaganda to Taliban: 'You Are Condemned,'" CNN. www.cnn.com.

James M. McMichael and Michael S. Francis, "Micro Air Vehicles—Toward a New Dimension in Flight," Defense Advanced Research Projects Agency. www.darpa.mil.

John McWethy, "Robo-Planes: Unmanned Aircraft Redefines How Military Wages War," ABC News. http://abcnews.go.com.

Mennonite Central Committee, "Clusters of Death." www.mcc.org.

Judith Miller and Eric Schmitt, "A Nation Challenged: Ugly Duckling Turns Out to Be Formidable in the Air," *New York Times,* November 23, 2001, Terrorism Project. www.cdi.org.

Nelson Mumma Jr., "Special Operations Improves M4 Carbine," Army News Service, ArmyLink, September 14, 1998. www.dtic.mil.

John B. Nathman, "'We Were Great': Navy Air in Afghanistan." *Proceedings,* U.S. Naval Institute, March 2002. www.usni.org.

Sean D. Naylor, "In Shah-E-Kot, Apaches Save the Day—and Their Reputation," *Army Times,* 21st Cavalry Brigade (Air Combat). www.hood.army.mil.

Amanda Onion, "Owning the Night," ABC News.com. http://abcnews.go.com.

Kris Osborn, "Air Force Seeks Deeper-Penetrating 'Bunker-Busters,'" CNN. www.cnn.com.

————, "Navy Seals Play Crucial Role in War on Terror," CNN. www.cnn.com.

PBS, "Campaign Against Terror," *Frontline.* www.pbs.org.

Frank Pelligrini, "What in the World Is Diego Garcia?" *Time.* www.time.com.

Charles Portman, "Green Berets Standing Up Afghan Army," ArmyLink. www.dtic.mil.

Kathleen T. Rehm, "Fliers Share Enduring Freedom Experiences at Andrews Open House," DC Military. www.dcmilitary. com.

Paul Richter, "U.S. Gunship Offers Awesome Firepower," *Los Angeles Times,* October 17, 2001, Global Security. www.global security.org.

Thomas E. Ricks, "U.S. Arms Unmanned Aircaft," *Washington Post,* SouthCoast Today, October 17, 2001. www.s-t.com.

Nic Robertson, "Meet Packbot: The Newest Recruit." CNN, August 10, 2002. www. cnn.com.

James G. Roche, "Salute to Air Commandos," speech at Andrews Air Force Base, U.S. Air Force, October 9, 2002. www.af.mil.

Donald Rumsfeld, "'The 21st Century' Transformation of the U.S. Armed Forces," DefenseLink, January 31, 2002. www.defense link.mil.

Tanalee Smith, "Robots Draw Rough Duty as U.S. Combat-Tests Them in Afghanistan," Associated Press, Space.com, July 30, 2002. www.space.com.

Kirk Spitzer, "Green Berets Outfought, Outthought the Taliban." *USA Today,* January 6, 2002. www.usatoday.com.

Terrorism Project, *International Herald Tribune,* December 28, 2001. www.cdi.org.

———, *New York Times,* November 23, 2001. www.cdi.org.

Bijal P. Trivedi, "U.S. Buys Up Afghanistan Images from Top Satellite," *National Geographic Today,* October 25, 2001. http://news.national geographic.com.

U.S. Navy Office of Information, ". . . From the Sea: Preparing the Naval Service for the 21st Century." www.chinfo.navy.mil.

Steve Vogel, "Gas Stations in the Sky Extend Fighters' Reach," *Washington Post,* November 1, 2001. www.washingtonpost. com.

Robert Wall, "Navy Adapts Operations for Afghan War Hurdles," *Aviation Week and Space Technology,* Aviation Now, November 19, 2001. www.aviationnow.com.

Paul Weisman, "Afghanistan Caves Thwart Invaders," *USA Today,* November 5, 2001. www.usatoday.com.

White House, "Address to a Joint Session of Congress and the American People." www.whitehouse.gov.

David Williams, "Pulverised by the Daisy Cutter," *War on Terror,* Associated News Media. www.femail.co.uk.

☆ Index ☆

AC-130 gunships, 33–34, 40
Adam, Eugene C., 27, 28
Advanced KH-11 (camera), 62–63
Aegis system, 20
Afghanistan
  air attacks on, 23
  aircraft carrier operations against, 22–24
  caves in, 42–43
  cities of, 22
  humanitarian aid efforts for, 48–49, 50, 51
  Northern Alliance allies and, 80
  radio broadcasts from aircraft and, 51–53
air bases, 12–13
airborne warning and control system aircraft (AWACS), 71
aircraft. *See* aircraft carriers; fighter aircraft; helicopters
aircraft carriers
  battle groups (CVBGs) of, 19–21
  dimensions and descriptions of, 16–17
  fighter jets and, 22–25
  importance of, 14
  nuclear power and, 15–16
  operations of, against Afghanistan, 22–24

support and protection for, 19–21
  weapons carried by, 17–19
air delivery boxes. *See* TRIADs
airdrops, 48–51
Air Force Special Operations Command (AFSOC), 83–85
Air Intelligence Agency, 51–53
Allen, Thomas B., 61
APG-71 (radar system), 25
armored vest, 90
Army Rangers, 74–76
Arnold, Henry H. "Hap," 83
A-Teams, 80–81
  see also Green Berets
Ault, Frank, 25
B-1B Lancers, 32–33
B-2 Spirit stealth bombers, 30–32
B-52 Stratofortress, 28–30
Bank, Aaron, 77
Beckwith, Charles, 77
bin Laden, Osama, 43, 66
Black Hawk. *See* helicopters, Black Hawk
BLUs (bomb live units), 38–41
Boeing Aircraft Company, 29, 49, 70
bombers, 28–34
  see also specific names

bomblets, 37–38
bombs, 35–44
  air force tactics for, 31
  CBU-87, 38–39
  cluster, 37–39
  Daisy Cutter, 39–41
  Mark 80, 35–37
  smart, 41–42, 64, 65
  thermobaric, 44
  unexploded, 37
Boone, Doug, 69–70
Brown, Doug, 75
Bunker Busters (GBU-28 smart bombs), 43–44
Bush, George W., 9, 10, 13

C-17 Globemaster III, 48–49, 51
C-130 Hercules, 51
Campbell, Duncan, 11
Carl Vinson (aircraft carrier), 14, 19, 21
CIA, 61, 67
Clancy, Tom, 19, 77–78
Clark, Wesley, 34
Clinton, Bill, 14
close-in weapons system (CIWS), 18–19
Cochie, Kevin, 59
cockpits, 27–28
Cold War, 13, 45, 60–61
combat clothing, 90–91
combat control teams (CCTs), 84–85
combat-support ships, 21

Commando Solo, 51–53
communications, jamming of, 54–56
Copple, John, 64
Corona, 60–61
cruisers, 19–21
CVW (carrier air wing), 22–23

Daly, Paul, 69
Defense Intelligence Agency (DIA), 61
DefenseLink, 94
Defense Meteorological Satellite Program, 66
Delta Force, 77
destroyers, 14, 19–20
Diego Garcia, 13, 29–30, 32

E-3 Sentry aircraft, 70–72
Eberhart, Ralph E., 65
electronic-countermeasures officers (ECMOs), 54–56
electronic-warfare systems, 19
see also bombs, smart; smart weapons
Enterprise (aircraft carrier), 15
explosives, 89

FBI, 61
fighter aircraft, 22–28
firearms. See specific names
First Special Forces Operational Detachment–Delta, 77
food drops, 48–49, 50
forward presence, 13–14
Francis, Michael S., 68
Franks, Tommy R., 11, 16

Frost, Tom, 96

glass cockpit, 27–28
Global Hawk (RQ-4A) surveillance aircraft, 69–70
Global Positioning System (GPS), 9, 41, 42, 64–65
Goldstein, Frank, 51
Green Berets
  Afghanistan missions of, 80–81
  creed of, 78
  history of, 77
  invisible operations of, 80
  motto of, 81
  qualifications of, 76–77
  training of, 77–79
grenades, 89, 90
Grumman Aircraft Corporation, 24
Guardian (newspaper), 11
guerrillas. See Delta Force; Green Berets
guided-missile cruisers, 19, 21
guided-missile destroyers, 14, 19–20
Guidry, Mike, 70
guns, 18–19

Handy, John W., 49, 51
helicopters, 56–59
  Apache (AH-64), 57–58
  Black Hawk (UH-60), 56–57
  Chinook (MH-47) transport, 58–59
  Cobra (AH-1), 57–58
  Pave Low, 56
  special-ops, 56
helmets, 90

Hoffman, Timothy, 31
homeland surveillance, 71
Hornets, 26–28
horses, 94
humanitarian daily rations (HDRs), 37, 49, 50, 71
humanitarian missions, 48–51, 71
Hydra folding fin rockets, 57

IKONOS (satellite), 63–64
infrared decoys, 19
intelligence, 60–66

jets. See fighter aircraft
Jette, Bruce, 95, 96–97
John C. Stennis (aircraft carrier), 19
John Paul Jones (aircraft carrier), 19–21
joint direct-attack munitions (JDAMs), 41–42, 64, 65
see also bombs, smart
joint tactical information distribution system (JTIDS), 25–26

Kelso, Michael, 76
Kevlar, 90, 91
Key West (submarine), 21
Keystone camera systems, 61–62
Kitty Hawk (aircraft carrier), 19, 80
Korean War, 9
Kosovo, 5
Kuwait, 13
Kwolek, Stephanie, 91

Lacrosse satellites, 65–66

LANTIRN (low-altitude navigation and targeting infrared), 26
laser markers, special-operations forces (SOFLAMs), 93
lasers, 92–95
laser target designators (LTDs), 93
leaflets, 52
Lockheed (aircraft), 51

M4 carbines, 88–90
M4A1 rifles, 89
M-9 Beretta pistol, 90
M-16 rifles, 87–88
machine guns, 89–90
MacIntyre, Jamie, 52
Mark 15 Phalanx, 18–19
Martens, Bob, 85
Martin, Mike, 84
Mathewson, Eric, 67
MAVs (micro air vehicles), 68
McDonnell Douglas, 27
McDonnell, Kevin, 81
McMichael, James M., 68
MC-130s, 40
mercy flights, 48–51
"Micro Air Vehicles—Toward a New Dimension in Flight" (McMichael and Francis) (report), 68
micro UAVs (micro unmanned aerial vehicles), 68
mines, 89
missiles, 17–18, 44–47, 55–56, 57
 cruise, 21, 45
 Hellfire antiarmor, 57, 69
 high-speed antiradiation

(HARMs), 55–56
intercontinental ballistic (ICBM), 45
Maverick (AGM-65 laser-guided), 46–47
Sea Sparrow (Mark 29), 17–18
Stinger, 41
Tomahawk cruise, 21, 44–46
Myers, Richard, 74, 76, 80

National Photographic Interpretation Center (NPIC), 61
National Reconnaissance Office (NRO), 61
National Security Agency (NSA), 61
Nautilus (submarine), 15
Naval Strike and Air Warfare Center (NSAWC), 25
Navstar satellites, 64–65
Newbold, Gregory S., 34
night-vision goggles (NVGs), 91–92
Northern Alliance, 12, 80

Olympia (submarine), 21
Oman, 13
Operational Detachment Alpha (ODA). See A-Teams
Operation Anaconda, 57–58, 82
Operation Enduring Freedom, 9, 13, 22

PASGT (personal armor system, ground troop), 90
Pearl Harbor, 7

Persian Gulf War, 9, 39–40, 43–44, 56, 80
pistols, 90
pod system, tactical airborne reconnaissance (TARPS), 26
Polmar, Norman, 61
precision-guided munitions, 41–47
Predator. See UAVs
Princeton (aircraft carrier), 19–20
propaganda, 51–53
protective clothing, 90–91
Prowler (EA-6B), 54–56
psychological operations (PSYOPs) missions, 51–53
Pushies, Fred J., 78

al-Qaeda
 aerial raids and, 69
 Afghanistan bunkers and, 42–43
 air strikes on, 73
 attack helicopters and, 58
 bombardment of, 12
 caves and, 95
 cluster bombs and, 38
 command centers of, 81
 identified, 9
 navy SEALs and, 82
 spy planes and, 67
Qatar, 13

radar-jamming, 54–56
radar systems, 19, 25–26
radio broadcasts, 51–53
Reagan, Ronald, 32
reconnaissance aircraft, 70–72
refueling aircraft, 53–54

Ricks, Thomas, 69
rifles, 86–90
robots, 95–97
Roche, James G., 84–85
rockets, 57
Rumsfeld, Donald, 10, 38, 94

Sacramento (combat-support ship), 21
satellites, 9
  radar-imaging, 65–66
  see also Global Positioning System (GPS); weather satellites
Saudi Arabia, 13
Schwarzkopf, Norman, 11, 16
SEALs, 82–83
Sea Sparrow. *See* missiles, Sea Sparrow
September 11, 2001, terrorist attacks, 7
Shepperd, Don, 44
sidearms, 80
signal intelligence satellites (SIGINT), 66
smart weapons, 41–47
Somalia, 5
Soviet Union, 43
Space Imaging Corporation, 63–64
Special Air Services (SAS), 77, 84
special forces. *See* Green Berets
Special Forces Assessment and Selection (SFAS), 78
special-operations forces.

See Green Berets
Spy Book: The Encyclopedia of Espionage (Polmar and Allen), 61
spy planes, 66–72
spying. *See* intelligence
squad automatic weapons (SAWs), 89–90
Stirling, David, 84
Stratotankers, 53–54
Stufflebeem, John, 31, 38, 72
submarines, 21

Taliban
  Army Rangers and, 76
  attack helicopters and, 58
  bombardment of, 12
  caves and bunkers of, 42–43, 94–95
  cluster bombs and, 38
  Green Berets and, 80
  identified, 9
  navy SEALs and, 82
  satellite intelligence photos and, 64
  spy planes and, 68
  Stinger of, 41
  U.S. bombing raids and, 34
tankers, 53–54
terminal guidance, 93
terrorists, 8–9, 58
  see also al-Qaeda
Theodore Roosevelt (aircraft carrier), 14, 19
Thompson, Andy, 31
Thunderbolts (A-10s), 34

Tomcats (F-14s), 24–26
Top Guns, 25
TRIADs (tri-walled air delivery boxes), 49
Tritonol, 43

UAVs (unmanned aerial vehicles), 66–70, 71
Underwater Demolition Teams (UDTs), 82
United States Central Command (CENTCOM), 16
U.S. Army Special Forces (Pushies), 78

Valle, J.C., 31
Vego, Milan, 12
Vietnam War
  bombing and, 33, 35, 39–40
  fighter pilots and, 25
  helicopters and, 58–59
  questions about, 5–6
  special forces and, 77
  weapons used in, 9

warships. *See* aircraft carriers; combat-support ships; cruisers; destroyers; *see also specific names*
weather satellites, 66
Wiercinski, Frank, 58
Williams, David, 40
World Trade Center, 13
World War II, 7–8
Wren, Richard, 26

Zelibor, Thomas, 21

★ Picture Credits ★

Cover Photo: Landov

© AFP/CORBIS, 33, 39, 88

AP/Wide World Photos, 20, 43, 50, 58, 65, 68, 95

© CORBIS, 28

© CORBIS SYGMA, 62, 63

Department of Defense photo by Airman Recruit Mara McCleaft, U.S. Navy, 24

Department of Defense photo by Petty Officer First Class Todd Cichonowicz, U.S. Navy, 15

Department of Defense photo by Petty Officer Third Class Alex C. Witte, U.S. Navy, 27

Department of Defense photo by R.D. Ward, 11

Department of Defense photo by Senior Airman Jeffrey Allen, U.S. Air Force, 53

Department of Defense photo by Staff Sgt. Jason Gamble, U.S. Air Force, 55

Department of Defense photo by Staff Sgt. Mary L. Smith, U.S. Air Force, 30

© Wally McNamee/CORBIS, 87

Brandy Noon, 12

Reuters/Steven James Silva/Landov, 8

© Leif Skoogfors/CORBIS, 79

U.S. Air Force photo by Staff Sgt. Jerry Morrison, 72

U.S. Air Force photo by Tech. Sgt. Scott Reed, 67

U.S. Army photo by Mitch Frazier, 75

U.S. Navy Photo, 81

U.S. Navy photo by Photographer's Mate Airman Apprentice Lance H. Mayhew Jr., 46

U.S. Navy photo by Photographer's Mate Airman John W. Blair, 92

U.S. Navy photo by Photographer's Mate First Class Tim Turner, 74, 83

U.S. Navy photo by Photographer's Mate Second Class Angela M. Virnig, 18

U.S. Navy photo by Photographer's Mate Second Class Corey T. Lewis, 36

U.S. Navy photo by Photographer's Mate Third Class Alta A. Cutler, 42

U.S. Navy photo by Photographer's Mate Third Class Martin S. Fuentes, 17

★ About the Author ★

Craig E. Blohm has been writing magazine articles on historical subjects for children for twenty years. He has also written for social studies textbooks and has conducted workshops in writing history for children. A native of Chicago, he has worked for more than twenty-five years in the field of television production as writer, producer, and director. He is currently the television and radio production coordinator at Purdue University, Calumet, in Hammond, Indiana. He and his wife, Desiree, live in Tinley Park, Illinois, and have two sons, Eric and Jason.